Hidden Greenwich
The Travel Guide

Phil Frampton

Published November 1999

ISBN 1 902167 02 3

MH*i*

Publications

Published by MHi Publications Ltd

44 Grindley Avenue Manchester M21 7NF

Photographs: front cover; Brian Crawford.
  inside; Brian Crawford and Ben Eastop
  except where stated.
Sketches and maps by Mark Gibbs.
Cover design by Ben Eastop. Design and page
  layout by Ben Eastop and Stuart Lawrence.
Researchers: Muriel Savrot and Chetan Patel.
Editors: Brian Crawford and Andrea Enisuoh.

The publishers wish to thank
Woolwich College for all their co-operation and
support with *Hidden Greenwich*.

Special thanks are also due to
Greenwich Local History Library,
Greenwich Tour Guides Association,
London Borough of Greenwich,
Jane Kinninmonth, Tim Ellis, Maureen Sinha,
Margy and Perminder,
Gail, Ellie and Sidonie Frampton.

Printed by Whitstable Litho, Whitstable, Kent

Contents

INTRODUCTION

Greenwich Borough

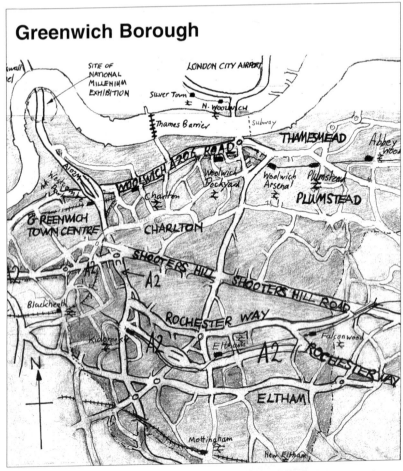

SITE OF NATIONAL MILLENIUM EXHIBITION

LONDON CITY AIRPORT

Silver Town

N. WOOLWICH

Thames Barrier

Subway

THAMESMEAD

Abbey Wood

WOOLWICH A206 ROAD

Woolwich Dockyard

Woolwich Arsenal

Plumstead

PLUMSTEAD

Charlton

GREENWICH TOWN CENTRE

CHARLTON

SHOOTERS HILL

SHOOTERS HILL ROAD

A2

A2

Blackheath

ROCHESTER WAY

Falconwood

ROCHESTER WAY

Kidbrooke

A2

Eltham

A2

N

ELTHAM

Mottingham

New Eltham

Greenwich in London

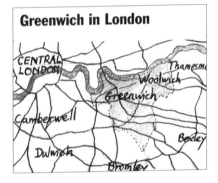

CENTRAL LONDON

Thamesmead

Woolwich

Greenwich

Camberwell

Bexley

Dulwich

Bromley

GREENWICH **More than a Dome**

Muriel and I had talked about Greenwich as a potentially pleasant tourist site with plenty of historic connections but to me it was simply another part of humdrum London. My travelling companion and I imagined it as merely another borough in the capital with no particularly distinctive features other than the site of the celebrated Millennium Dome. How wrong could we be? Having now spent much time in the borough, we agreed that it is one of the hidden gems of Britain. Situated on the Thames, it is speckled with historic royal palaces, mansions, woodland parks and wide ancient commons.

Greenwich Means Time

In 1884 an international conference agreed that Greenwich Mean Time would be the central axis for world time. A line linking the north and south poles through Greenwich would divide the world between East and West. Greenwich would be at 0 degrees longitude. All other lands would be defined as east or west of Greenwich. The Equator, a 24,000-mile imaginary line around the circumference of the earth equidistant from the North and South Poles, was defined as 0 degrees latitude, dividing the Northern Hemisphere from the Southern Hemisphere.

The international decision to mark Greenwich as 'the centre of time' reflected the area's maritime traditions. For the daily fall of the red time-ball on top of Greenwich Royal Observatory set the time for those British ships, which sailed down the Thames to dominate the oceans of the world.

Greenwich boasts the National Maritime Museum as one of the capital's finest monuments to Britain's sea-faring traditions and life in Greenwich borough was a key part of those traditions. Less is known by even the people of these isles of the historic role of Greenwich in the nation's development.

The British government has made Greenwich the centre of the country's millennium celebrations. But the country is generally unaware of the palaces and pastures of the area, recording almost 1,000 years of royal history. For almost a millennium, this spot by the Thames saw a procession of rulers of England. The kings Harold, Edward the Conqueror, Henry VIII, Charles I and George IV and queens Mary and Elizabeth I and the peoples' rebellions of Wat Tyler, Jack Cade and the Cornish peasants are all part of the Greenwich story. Fortunately some of the finest artistic creativity of those times remain, making Greenwich a must for visitors interested in history and culture.

At the Woolwich Arsenal, the Dockyards and the Royal Military Academy, the area also boasts links with the creation of the military might which gave birth to the largest empire the world will ever see. The officers and guns with which Britain secured military domination of two thirds of the world hailed from Greenwich Borough. Written into the Greenwich tale are General James Wolfe, Admiral Horatio Nelson, General Gordon, Lord Kitchener and Field Marshall Sir Garnet Wolseley. While no lovers of the aims of the British Empire and its enslavement of peoples, we could nevertheless find wonder in the epic story of sweat, heroism, sacrifice, greed and tragedy which shaped much of the world we see today.

A Mean Time in Greenwich

There is no better area in London for reflecting Britain's incredible history. But Greenwich is more than history. We stood by the Old Royal Observatory in Greenwich Royal Park looking across the River Thames to the city of London. We were but four miles from the centre of the capital. Yet we were set apart. That is the magic of Greenwich. I have spent some time living in the capital but Greenwich has its own special character.

The area still boasts much of the woodlands that formed the royal hunting grounds giving the districts a leafy suburban, sometimes almost rustic atmosphere and offering beautiful tranquil 'country' walks. This separation from the capital made sovereigns attempt to make Greenwich the Versailles of London and its inhabitants retain a pride in their history. As Versailles was a place for court society to relax, in Greenwich we found people with a little more time, a little more laid back then the normal stressed out Londoner. It meant we could enjoy not just the sites but the people.

With the Cutty Sark sailing ship, trips on the river to the Thames Barrier, palaces, woods, museums and fashionable shops there's plenty to do during the day. At nights we found bustling restaurants, concerts, pubs and clubs to keep even the keenest socialite busy. Although within easy access of London's famous West End nightlife, the beauty of Greenwich for us was that we could have a great night out in the area without having to spend a long time on

public transport or a huge amount on taxi fares getting home.

With lots to do for the kids, plenty of scenic views, places to eat and drink, packed full of history with its accompanying tales of chivalry, tragedy, horror and ghosts, Greenwich can certainly guarantee visitors a 'mean time'. So whether or not one goes to the Millennium Dome with its fantastic array of exhibitions make sure you enjoy Greenwich and see why it can justifiably claim to be one of Britain's most historic and attractive boroughs.

The Making of Greenwich

Climate and Geography

Visitors can expect warm temperate summers with temperatures between 16°C and 23°C and cool temperate winters with temperatures around 7°C, only occasionally cold enough to allow snow to settle. Greenwich is just six miles from central London. The area nearest to the Thames is reclaimed marshland while further from the river the area rises onto a plateau looking over into Kent and south east England.

Average monthly temperatures and rainfall in London

	Jan	Feb	Mar	April	May	June	July	Aug	Sep	Oct	Nov	Dec
Temp °C	4	5	7	9	12	16	18	17	15	11	8	5
Rainfall mm	54	40	37	37	46	45	57	59	49	57	64	48

History

The area around Greenwich sustained many small tribes prior to the Roman invasion. Beside the fish rich rivers and with plenty of arable land above the marsh area, it attracted many settlers. When the Romans came and developed London as their capital, the area again prospered.

The Romans left in the early 5th century, issuing in the Dark Ages and London's decline. Britain was split into warring factions headed by lords who sought alliances not only in England but also with foreign rulers. Consequently, despite becoming home for the country's sovereigns, from the 10th century much of Greenwich paid taxes to Flemish monks in what is now Belgium for 400 years.

When Harold was defeated and killed by the Norman invaders under William the Conqueror, it laid the seeds for Greenwich's rise to fortune. The new king, William I united England under one ruler and set up capital in London. Europe began to emerge from the Dark Ages with the Catholic Church as a major prop to the rule of the kings, princes and emperors. As London developed, so too did Greenwich and its surrounding areas due to the area being on the edge of London and on the major road to Dover and Europe.

The kings and queens set up palace away from the busy capital in the peace of the Eltham countryside. Later under Henry VII, they moved to Greenwich and the Palace of Placentia. Placentia was the favourite palace of Henry VIII until he moved to the newly developed Hampton Court. Elizabeth I also spent much time there.

Sir Frances Drake

Situated close to London, far enough down the Thames to make floating ships easy and far enough up to offer some protection from foreign marauders, the Royal Naval Dockyards of Deptford and Greenwich were ordered to be set up by Henry VIII. They would build the warships to defend the seas and take advantage of the growing world trade in products. Woolwich was called, "Mother of All Dockyards," and played a key part in the growth of the slave trade and the British Empire.

Under Elizabeth I, Sir John Hawkins and Sir Francis Drake set forth in Greenwich built boats, which would position Britain at the forefront of the growing slave trade. The coffers of the queen were swelled with this blood money. Both Hawkins and Drake had long connections with Woolwich shipyard with Drake having had his boats built there. In the 18th century almost 50 ships built at Woolwich and Deptford ploughed the Caribbean Sea to prop up the slave trade.

The merchants and plantation owners of Greenwich grew rich and the area continued to prosper particularly after the Great Plague had diminished the appeal of London. Royal courtiers flocked to Greenwich and Blackheath right up until the early 19th century. When Greenwich went out of royal fashion, it still prospered through the growing maritime trade and the fruits of empire.

Tradition was maintained with the now elected rulers of the country regularly visiting Greenwich, particularly for the annual Whitebait dinners which drew prime ministers and their cabinet colleagues to dine by the river bank – a tradition which has been re-established. One of Britain's greatest foreign statesmen, William Gladstone, stood to be elected for parliament in Greenwich.

Woolwich, with ample marshland providing some safety, was developing as the home of the Royal Ordnance, preparing the explosive power for the British military. The 19th century saw Britain's European rivals fighting for their share of the exploitation of the southern continents. The Royal Ordnance grew as the Arsenal and the Royal Artillery were stationed close by. At the Royal Military Academy, Woolwich became sister academy to Sandhurst College, training the elite officers of the British military. General Gordon and Lord Kitchener passed through the ranks.

Wars brought tens of thousands of people to work at the Arsenal. When the wars ended, Greenwich and the Arsenal went into decline. Nevertheless the recent rise in London's fortunes has given it a new lease of life. Today the area is one of modern history. Holding back the flood tides at Charlton is the Thames Barrier with the biggest movable barriers in the world. As a fitting tribute to the area's seafaring tradition, the National Maritime Museum in Greenwich is one of the largest maritime museums in the world and the Millennium Dome in North Greenwich boasts the biggest dome in the world.

Greenwich's regal history has ensured a legacy of many important monuments, buildings, the flora and fauna rich royal park and former royal hunting grounds. But the town also has a history of revolt and rebellion, Blackheath being the assembling ground for Wat Tyler's Poll Tax rebels, Jack Cade's Men of Kent and the Cornish Peasants' Revolt. The people's right to use common land was fought for at Plumstead Common where 20,000 came to protest at the imprisonment of commons' defender John de Morgan. Patriarchs, matriarchs, plebeians and paupers all played a part in shaping Greenwich as it is today. All have left their mark.

At the Centre Of Time

In ancient times, travellers would calculate their position on the earth by means of landmarks and the position of the Moon, Sun and stars. These crude measures sufficed while travel passed along familiar routes. As humankind's ability to travel the oceans increased so the old methods became outdated. Distances from the North and South Poles could easily be determined by reference to the Pole stars and the Sun. Latitude could therefore be determined quite precisely. Assessing longitude provided a much more difficult problem.

Once scientists finally agreed that the world was round they could start trying to calculate means of assisting navigation. They knew that if the earth took 24 hours to revolve one full circle on its axis then it would revolve 15 degrees in one hour of a 24-hour day. The Sun would therefore be at a certain point in the sky. However life was still not so simple and navigation remained hazardous.

In the early 1500s a scientist had proposed a means of assessing longitude by calculating the moon's position in relation to particular stars. By 1676 the Greenwich Observatory had been erected, with John Flamsteed as the Royal Astronomer charged with drawing up tables predicting the Moon's likely position.

In October 1707 four British naval ships were heading towards the entrance to the English Channel when they ran aground, with the loss of 2,000 sailors. The navigators had thought that they had reached the entrance to the Channel

The Normans

William I	1066-1087	William the Conqueror
William II	1087-1100	Rufus, 2nd son of William I
Henry I	1100-1135	3rd son of William I
Stephen	1136-1154	

The Plantagenets

Henry II	1154-1189	
Richard I	1189-1199	Richard the Lionheart
John	1199-1216	Brother of Richard
Henry III	1216-1272	Son of John
Edward I	1272-1307	Son
Edward II	1307-1327	Son
Edward III	1327-1377	Son
Richard II	1377-1399	Grandson Edward III, Son of the Black Prince, Deposed
Henry IV	1399-1413	House of Lancaster
Henry V	1413-1422	Son
Henry VI	1422-1461	Deposed
Edward IV	1461-1483	House of York
Edward V	1483-1483	The prince in the Tower
Richard III	1483-1485	Brother of Edward IV

Tudors

Henry VII	1485-1509	Married Elizabeth of York
Henry VIII	1509-1547	Married Anne Boleyn, Anne of Cleves, Jane Seymour, Katharine etc.
Edward VI	1547-1553	Son of Jane Seymour
Mary I	1553-1558	Daughter of Katharine of Aragon
Elizabeth I	1558-1603	Daughter of Anne Boleyn

Stuarts

James I	1603-1625	Also James VI of Scotland
Charles I	1625-1649	Younger son, Beheaded

Rulers of the Commonwealth Protectorate Republic

Oliver Cromwell	1653-1658	Leader of Parliament in English Civil War
Richard Cromwell	1658-1659	Resigned

Restoration of the Monarchy

Stuarts

Charles II	1660-85	Son of Charles I
James II	1685-1688	Also James VII of Scotland, Deposed

The Interregnum 1688-1689 The Glorious Revolution

William III & Mary II	1689-1694	
William III	1694-1702	
Anne	1702-1707	Younger sister of Mary

In 1707 England and its territories in Wales, Scotland and Ireland became the United Kingdom

Monarchs of the United Kingdom 1707- 1999

Stuarts Anne   1707-1714

Hanoverians

George I	1714-1727	Great grandson of James II
George II	1727-1760	Son of George I
George III	1760-1820	Grandson of George II
George IV	1820-1830	Son of George III, Became Prince Regent in 1811
William IV	1830-1837	Brother of George IV
Victoria	1837-1901	Daughter of Duke of Kent

House of Saxe-Coburg

Edward VII	1901-1910	Son

House of Windsor

George V	1910-1936	Son
Edward VIII	1936-1936	Son, abdicated
George VI	1936-1952	Son of George V
Elizabeth II	1952-........	Daughter

but their ships were in fact off the Scilly Isles. It sparked a national debate and by 1714 Parliament had passed a bill offering £20,000 to whoever could devise an accurate means of determining longitude at sea.

A John Harrison finally claimed the £20,000. His lifelong study of marine chronometers had paid off.

By 1766 work at the Greenwich Royal Observatory in relation to lunar-distance paid off. It enabled the production of the first Nautical Almanac, with the Moon's relative position calculated in relation to Greenwich, showing longitudes to the east and west. Britain, with its growing empire, ruled the seas and the Almanac became the major reference of the

Henry VIII

world. As maritime trade vastly expanded and new world powers began to emerge, the question of longitude and time required a universal solution.

In 1884 an international conference was convened in Washington to decide the issues. Other observatories existed in Washington DC, Berlin and Paris. Many other locations were put forward such as the Pyramids of Egypt, the Temple of Jerusalem and the Azores and the debate raged for a fortnight. However Britain controlled world trade and three-quarters of the oceans' ships were already using Greenwich as their prime meridian. Greenwich finally won the vote to be the location of the universally accepted prime meridian. The vote was not unanimous. France and Brazil abstained and San Domingo voted against Greenwich.

At the same conference Greenwich also became the centre of time for the universal day. Earth's daytime officially would begin, "for all the world at the moment of mean midnight of the initial meridian."

Paris Mean Time

France had voted with Brazil and Santo Domingo for Paris to become the prime meridian at the 1884 international conference. In Paris the French had their own observatory which marked time 20 minutes ahead of GMT.

After 1789 the republic had been determined to establish a universal measure as part of a general search for unity in all matters. The meridian eventually became a Gallic line stretching north and south through Paris.

French rivalry with England remained with the hotting up of the drive to colonise Africa and other parts of the globe. France continued to advance Paris Mean Time for 27 years until 1911 when the republic abandoned its lone struggle.

However the Gallic Line will be re-introduced as part of France's millennium celebrations when on July 14th three million citizens will be invited to one massive party along the route. The line will be marked out with 960 km of olives, oaks and yews. On December 31st the French are expected to celebrate the new millennium 20 minutes earlier than in the UK.

Greenwich Today

Today's Greenwich is a marvellous combination of a city suburb, the semi-rusticism of the river plain and undulating hill plateaux. The borough comprises the districts of Greenwich, Blackheath, Charlton, Eltham, Plumstead, Woolwich and Thamesmead. Uniting them are the woodlands of Shooters Hill. The river plain, formerly marshland, is a busy industrial area while inland the area has plenty of beautiful woodlands and green open spaces.

Properties are much sought after in Blackheath and Greenwich and the advent of the tube connection to London will boost the area's attractiveness. The trendiest shopping area of the borough is without doubt Blackheath, with Greenwich closely following. But each of the other areas has plenty of attractions and the advantage of being less pricey.

Thamesmead is the most easterly and newest part of the borough, having been built on 1500 acres of former marshland in a government project begun in the 1960s.

The borough has an elected council with the Labour Party being the main political party. Baron Greenwich is none other than HRH Prince Philip, husband to the Queen of England.

Being there – what's to do

Manners

'Please' and 'thank you' are still the best words in the English dictionary. A smile is the best expression. London is very cosmopolitan so take care to speak clearly and precisely in order to be understood. Shaking hands is still common though it is trendy nowadays to exchange hugs or pecks on the check, French style. Queuing for transport is still common and queue jumpers frowned upon. "Manners," said Roosevelt, "are a thousand petty sacrifices." Most people will appreciate you for holding doors open for them, helping those with awkward loads get off public transport and being aware that giving a little time can make others' lives more bearable and your own more pleasant.

Palaces and Mansions

With its regal history Greenwich has plenty of palaces, garrisons, fine halls and mansions of artistic and historic interest dotted around the borough. **Queen's House**, the **National Maritime Museum** and the **Royal Naval College** are in Greenwich. **Rangers House, McCartney House, Morden College** and **The Paragon** are in Blackheath. **Eltham Palace, Well Hall Tudor Barn, Eltham Lodge** and **Avery Hill** are in Eltham. **The Royal Military Academy**, the **Royal Artillery Barracks** and the Garrison church are in Woolwich and **Charlton House** is in Charlton.

Parks, Woods and Open Spaces

With **Greenwich Royal Park**, **Blackheath** and **Oxleas Wood,** Greenwich is one of London's most blessed boroughs for parks, woodland and open space. Greenwich Royal Park is the oldest royal park in London and the most scenic. But the borough also boasts many other old parks including **Charlton Park, Maryon-Wilson Park** in Charlton and **Middle Park** in Eltham. We found the ancient woodland and hunting grounds of **Oxleas Wood, Jack Wood, Castle Wood, Eltham Common** and **Shepherdleas Wood** quite magical, offering splendid walks away from the crowds and bustle of the capital.

More formal parks include **Maryon Park** in Charlton and **Eltham Park North** and **South. Plumstead Common** offers lovely open spaces, as does **Woolwich Common**, still formally owned by the Army but open to the public for 364 days a year. **Thamesmead Marshes** once owned by the Royal Arsenal have acres of marshland offering pleasant walks and a surprising treat for nature lovers.

Maritime Greenwich and Trips on the Thames River

The history of Greenwich is linked to British maritime history. Woolwich Dockyard was the site of Henry VIII's Royal Dockyard. The **Trafalgar Tavern** on the waterfront close to Greenwich Pier was an old sailors' haunt and entertained the likes of **Admiral Horatio Nelson** and his right hand man, 'Kiss Me' Hardy. Beside the pier stands the old tea clipper, the **Cutty Sark**, with its tall masts. Next door is the **Gypsy Moth IV**, the first boat to be sailed single-handedly around the world.

Great Architects and Sculptors in Greenwich

With Greenwich having such a regal history, it comes as no surprise to find the works of some of Britain's great artists littered throughout the borough. Of these the most notable works are those of the architects Sir Christopher Wren, Nicholas Hawksmoor, Sir John Vanbrugh, James 'Athenian' Stuart and Inigo Jones.

***Sir Christopher Wren** (1632-1723) is best known for design-ing St Paul's Cathedral but many of his other designs appear throughout London. Also an artist and astronomer he designed an interior in the Old Royal Observatory. His classical buildings include The Royal Naval College in Greenwich, Kensington Palace, Chelsea Royal Hospital and the east wing of Hampton Court.*

*The Baroque **Nicholas Hawksmoor** (1661-1736) worked with Wren on the Royal Naval College. Hawksmoor is known for the outstanding individuality and eccentricity in his work. He also designed St Alfege's Church in Greenwich and Conduit Head in the Royal Park.*

***Sir John Vanbrugh** (1664-1726) was a restoration architect and while follower of Wren, also worked with Hawksmoor. He was involved with the Royal Naval College and other designs include Blenheim Palace, Castle Howard and possibly buildings in the Woolwich Arsenal.*

***Inigo Jones** (1573-1652) was to the fore in the British Classical revival in design. His works include Queen's House in Greenwich, Queen's Chapel at St James, the Banquetting House in Whitehall and a summer house in Charlton House.*

***James 'Athenian' Stuart** (1713-1788) designed the chapel in the Royal Naval College. A student of Ancient Greece, his designs often feature Greek motifs.*

*Among the sculptors whose work features in the borough are **Nicholas Stone** (1586-1647), the foremost British sculptor of the 17th century, **Sir Francis Chantrey** (1781-1841) the principal sculptor of the Georgian period whose works include the statue of George IV in Trafalgar Square, sculptor and woodcarver, **Grinling Gibbons** (1648-1721) who worked with Wren and the outstanding modern British sculptor, **Henry Moore** (1898-1989) whose work can be seen in Greenwich Park.*

The sailors' timepiece, the **Old Royal Observatory** stands at the top of Greenwich Park. To get a view of the river life it's worth taking the ferry down to the **Thames Barrier** – said to be the eighth wonder of the world and a vital part of London's flood defences, stopping the river side from reverting to salt marshes. Sergeant's boats also travel up river to Westminster and the Houses of Parliament home to the national assembly elected to govern Britain.

Walks

The Riverside Walk now offers a seven-mile continuous walk from Greenwich to Woolwich along the south bank of the Thames. There are also several **Green Chain Walks** taking in the woods around Shooters Hill. **Tour guides** from **Greenwich Tour Guide Association** organise a number of interesting walks around the borough. These include children's walks, ghost walks, health walks and bicycle tours. Greenwich Tour Guides can currently be found at Greenwich Pier. Green Chain Walks cross all points of the district and these guidebooks can be found in **Greenwich Tourist Information Centre.**

Museums

Pride of place goes to the **National Maritime Museum** but the area has other museums with fascinating collections on display. They include the **Fan Museum** in Greenwich, the Rangers House with its Suffolk Art Collection in Blackheath, **Greenwich Borough Local History Museum** in Plumstead and the **Greenwich Local History Library** in Woodlands, which also houses Blackheath's **Woodlands Art Gallery.** The **National Maritime Museum** has many of its 4,000 oil paintings on show and the **Citizens' Gallery** in Woolwich has a varied programme of exhibitions. Sir James Thornhill's (1675-1734) baroque mural on the ceiling of the Painted Hall in the **Royal Naval College** is one of his finest paintings.

Sports and Other Recreations

Blackheath boasts the oldest **rugby club** in the world and the oldest **golf club** in Britain. The heath attracted kings, lords and ladies to sport and today it's still a place where one can play soccer, cricket, go kart sailing, boating and the like. For spectator sports the borough has **Charlton Athletic Football Club**, **Blackheath Rugby Club** and **Blackheath & Eltham Golf Club**. **Rowing** is also popular on the Thames and again Blackheath has one of the oldest boat clubs.

Swimming baths open to the public include **Eltham Pools**, Eltham Hill (0208 850 4756) and **Thamesmere** and **Waterfront** Leisure Centres. **Yachting** and boating facilities are available at the **Lakeside Centre** on Southmere Lake in Thamesmead.

Leisure centres include; **Arches**, Trafalgar Rd, Greenwich (tel 0208 317 5000), **Meadowside**, Tudway Rd, Kidbrooke (0208 856 0101), **Plumstead**, Speranza St, Plumstead (tel 0208 855 8289), **Thamesmere**, Thamesmere Drive, Thamesmead (tel 0208 311 1119), **Elm Terrace Fitness Centre**, Messeter Place, Eltham (0208 850 1234) and **The Waterfront**, High St, Woolwich (tel 0208 317 5000).

Eating Out

There are plenty of places to eat out in Greenwich ranging from pub grub to fine restaurants. Around Greenwich High Road, Greenwich Church Street and Nelson Road Greenwich town has an array of restaurants and cafes offering English, French, Thai, Vietnamese, Mexican and fast food.

Halomama's noodle bar, **The North Pole** on Greenwich High Rd and the vegetarian restaurant, **Googies**, are all popular. Blackheath Village is a gourmet's delight with over 20 restaurants offering a wide variety of menus. Of these, **Lawn Terrace** and **Chapter Two** are two of the most upmarket restaurants in the borough. The new **Cave Austen** is situated close by.

Zap on Eltham High St serves good Anglo-French food with **Mellins** offering an atmospheric alternative.

Over in Charlton, a handy place to eat is **Floyds Bar** in Charlton Athletic's football stadium. There are a couple of Tandoori restaurants in the village and the **Thames Barrier Visitors Centre** has a café. For a choice of Indian takeaways, Plumstead High St beside the **Woolwich Islamic Mosque** is definitely worth a visit.

Entertainment – Pubs and Clubs

Greenwich has plenty of pubs, many of which serve pub grub at reasonable prices. Pubs generally open around 10.30am staying open till 11pm at night. On Sundays pubs open at noon and may close at 2pm, re-opening in the evenings until 10.30pm. Several pubs are listed in the guide as holding weekly pub quiz competitions, which are open to all to enter. Others have live music events which are also listed. **Folk music** and **jazz** can be found in Greenwich at the **Cricketers Arms** and more jazz at **The Cactus Pit** and **Lawn** in Blackheath Village and the **Cricketers**.

Trendy venues include **Time Gallery** in Greenwich, **Cave Austin** in Blackheath village and **The Ordnance Club** in Market Square, Woolwich. Charlton has several pubs popular with young people including **The Angerstein**, **The Lord Napier** and **Pickwicks**.

Dance clubs include **Flamingos** frequented by local over 25s, The **Ordnance Cub** in Market Square, Woolwich and the **Paradise Bar** reggae club.

Blackheath Concert Halls is the area's premier concert venue with music ranging from classical through opera to folk and hip-hop. Other concert venues include **Woolwich Public Halls** and **St Alfege Church.** The Lawn in Blackheath hosts jazz on Mondays.

Among the crop of current Greenwich musicians, **Jools Holland** and his **Rhythm & Blues Orchestra** are probably the most notable. Jools outstanding boogie woogie piano and rhythm and blues launched him into a whirl of fame as one of Britain's most respected musicians, songwriters and television presenters.

Greenwich has its own cosy and popular **Greenwich Theatre** and the **Princes Theatre**. Eltham has the **Bob Hope Theatre** while theatrical performances are also put on at **Blackheath Concert Halls** and **The Age Reminiscence Centre** in Blackheath. **Greenwich Dance Agency** stages dance performances.

Some of London's best comedy is served up at **Up The Creek** comedy club hosted by one of the fathers of Britain's current batch of alternative comedians, **Malcolm Hardy**.

Festivals

Christmas and New Year will see major festivals as is traditional in England. In addition, Greenwich also holds its own special festivals, the biggest of which is the **Greenwich & Docklands International Festival** held in July of each year. The festival begins and ends with spectacular fireshows while theatre, dance and a whole range of musical performances take place throughout the week. The events are spread across the borough's main venues and into Docklands on the north side of the Thames.

In July, Greenwich holds a major **anti-racist festival** as well as a **jazz festival.** On a more traditional note, in October, Charlton hosts the **Hornfair**, a traditional festival whose origin is said to go back to the time of Robin Hood and King John.

What's Going On?

There are several free listings magazines detailing what's on at the various venues. These include the monthly **Meridian Line** and **The Guide**, the **South London Press**, **The Mercury** and **News Shopper**. For other information you can visit the Greenwich Tourist Information Office or the **New Millennium Experience** office at Greenwich Pier.

What to Buy?

Greenwich has two thriving markets in its centre with plenty of bargains on offer, including all manner of antiques. As one might expect Greenwich is a fine place for picking up maritime memorabilia and has plenty of such shops around Greenwich Church St. For really trendy and expensive shopping visitors should go to Blackheath. Woolwich has a busy shopping centre, with a weekday market for fruit and vegetables, flowers and household goods. And what about money? All over Greenwich we found plenty of cash machines. Cash cards were by far the safest and easiest way of taking care of our money. Remember when travelling by bus to take plenty of change, as notes can be difficult for drivers to exchange. Travel cards (for bus, train and tube from stations and newsagents) are good value and convenient.

Where To Stay

The best way to sample the delights of Greenwich is to find accommodation in the area. Until recently Greenwich suffered from a serious lack of accommodation for visitors but, since the Millennium Dome was erected, that is beginning to change.

Hotels

Hotels range from the small but expensive **Bardon Lodge** at £75 per night to the £27 a night en suite rooms at **Meadowcroft Lodge** in Eltham. The **Ibis** and **Clarendon** are also in the £50 plus range while **Greenwich Parkhouse** and the **Mitre** offer medium range prices. For a busy thriving hotel with lots of entertainment and activities, try the **Clarendon**. Alternatively, for a quieter stay, try **Bardon Lodge**. The Clarendon is excellently situated in Blackheath on the edge of the heath while the Mitre is located close to the Cutty Sark. If the accommodation close to the Dome is booked up, it's worth trying **Weston House** or **Yardley Court** beside Eltham Palace (see listings).

Bed & Breakfast

Bed and Breakfast places are increasing and are included in the listings in the back of the book. All those listed have been checked by the London Tourist Board except those with ETB Applied next to them. Prices range from £15 a night to £60 a night though most prices are around £20 to £25 per night per person. Many B&Bs are non-smoking. We also include details on the few places available for self-catering accommodation.

Camping

Abbey Wood Caravan Club (0208 310 2233 fax 311 6007) on Federation Rd in Abbey Wood offers the nearest accommodation for those wishing to camp out or take their caravan to see Greenwich.

Youth Hostels

The nearest youth hostel to Greenwich is **Rotherhithe Youth Hostel** (0207 232 2114) on Salter Rd in SE16. Otherwise **Binnie Court** (0208 694 2789) on Greenwich High Rd takes **young people** at £15 a night.

Kids Greenwich

Greenwich has plenty to offer children on holiday or just visiting the area. Here we outline some of the highlights and some of the practical places that children might want to visit. We have divided up the places into those under shelter and those mainly indoors and include a few suggestions for what to do during the evenings. Those places marked * have a restaurant or snack bar. The listings section to the back of this book also includes a list of summer courses and activities for children run by Greenwich Leisure.

Greenwich Under Shelter

Greenwich Town

From the Cutty Sark take a boat trip to the Thames Barrier. Hear an old sea captain recite the story of the Thames while cruising past the Dome, river birds and ships to the huge Thames Barrier that stops London flooding. Plenty of fun interactive games for all ages and lots of old boats can be found at the **National Maritime Museum**.* Children's entry is free. Touch base on the **Meridian Line** and see old telescopes and timepieces at the **Old Royal Observatory** in **Greenwich Park**. Children's entry is free. Beside the park on Croom Hill is the delightful **Fan Museum***.

In the village, **Greenwich Market*** has lots of stalls selling interesting items. **The Dome** has fantastic interactive games, learning experiences and has theatre, cinema, shows and restaurants. Greenwich has plenty of restaurants. The **Odeon** on High St shows the latest **movies.**

Blackheath

Blackheath Concert Halls stage children's theatre and all sorts of musical performances. An interesting place is the **Age Exchange Centre***. Located near the train station the centre has numerous items on display which were part of people's lives over 50 years ago. Blackheath has plenty of up-market restaurants.

Charlton

Charlton House in The Village is a great place to visit for those who like ghost stories and want to know more about royalty. Charlton is also the site of the Thames Barrier*. Close by is a **Russian Submarine** that you can go inside. **Charlton Athletic*** offer a tour of the soccer club and the ground detailing its history and players. Alternatively you can always go to watch the matches. Near Charlton train station is a Macdonald's.

Woolwich

The **Woolwich Free Ferry** crosses from Woolwich to the north bank of the Thames where there is a railway museum. You can ride the ferry all day because it's free. *The Rotunda Museum* has a great display of old cannons and guns. *Woolwich Odeon* shows current movies. Teenagers might wish to take a trip to *The Place* (0208 316 7533) at 32A Hare St in Woolwich. The Place is a young people's project based around a café and featuring cyberfights, graffiti meetings and other adventurous programmes.

Eltham

Eltham has the ancient Eltham Palace. In the town centre are a few restaurants and a McDonald's.

Plumstead

Greenwich Borough Museum on Plumstead High St takes you back through the area's development over 5,000 years with finds from archaeological digs, models and detailed explanations about how the Romans, Anglo Saxons, kings, queens and peasants lived all those years ago.

Mainly outdoors

Every part of Greenwich has a large amount of green open spaces. Most parks have children's play areas with swings, slides and other rides.

In Greenwich, the three-masted *Cutty Sark* sailing ship from the Victorian era is worth a look over above and below deck and nearby is the yacht of *Sir Francis Chichester*, *Gypsy Moth IV.*

Greenwich Park has a **deer park**, a boating pond and plenty of picnic space*. In Blackheath, the **heath** has a **boating pond** and acres of space for **kite flying**, **soccer, cricket** and go-karting. Shooters Hill is most famous for its magical Oxleas Wood that has a large open space popular for picnics.*

Maryon Wilson Park in Charlton has a children's **zoo** situated in beautiful woodland. Woolwich has the large Woolwich Common. Close to Eltham Place are *The Tarn*, home for a large number of ducks, and Middle Park. *Winn's Common* in Plumstead is a fine place for a picnic with spectacular views over the Thames.

Thamesmead Marshes have plenty of **wildlife** and interesting bits of the old Royal Arsenal site hidden in the undergrowth. The Lakeside Centre on Southmere Lake has yachting and boating facilities and lots of ducks eager to be fed. Close by are the ruins of Lesnes Abbey set in pleasant surrounds besides Abbey Wood.

INTRODUCTION

Greenwich Tour Guide Association's Ghost Tour

Greenwich Tour Guide Association offers tailored tours for children. We found the Ghost Tour to be one of the highlights – not too scary but very interesting and educational for the kids. To test out the Ghost Tour we sent researchers Lucy Welton (aged 10), Amy Welton (7), Rebecca Hall (9), Sarah Hall (7) and Rachel Hall (5) on the tour. Lucy sent us her comments.

On the Ghost Tour by Lucy Welton (aged 10).

"First we went to St Alfege's church. The bishop was held for ransom by the Vikings, imprisoned in Canterbury Cathedral. The Vikings had a drunken orgy and threw ox bones at the bishop. One put the bishop out of his misery by killing him with an axe right where he was talking. This scared Rebecca and me.

Then we walked to the market. Now it sells most things but it used to be a live-stock and vegetable market. I've been there before. It's quite enjoyable. My mum would say, 'I go there for brilliant bargains. I buy all the deals'.

Then we heard about gravediggers who dig out dead bodies for doctors and scientists to experiment on. The guide Jerry actually made my face green by saying that some people were buried so soon that when they were dug up they were a little alive.

Then we went to the Cutty Sark and heard about the 'Hell Voyage'. The Cutty Sark's captain and first mate were so cranky that the crew left. They pulled out all the young men from the docks to be sailors but had no experience. One boy called Billy Francis had a fight with the first mate. So the mate threw an iron rod at Billy. Billy died in three days. It made me quite sad but it is history.

Soon the captain got really cranky and went to the ships carpenter one day at four o'clock in the morning. 'Where's the second mate?' 'On deck captian.'

When he got on deck the second mate saw him but then a dark cloud went overhead. When it cleared the captain disappeared! The crew put a small boat over the side. They didn't find him only the outline of sharks in the dismal, murky waters. Nobody ever saw him again but around eight years ago the ship's cook got up on a blazing sunny day but then got very cold. He saw a faint shadow as grey as a damp street with old crumbling houses.

'Did you see that?' he asked as one crew members walked in.

'Yes.'

Was it the captain? Was it Billy Francis? Nobody knows. Keep your eyes peeled if you go there. I'm warning you. If you go to the Cutty Sark be prepared for sudden coldness and grey shadows.

'Why is it called Cutty Sark?' asked my younger sister Amy.

'A famous poet called Robbie Byrns in Scotland wrote a poem about a farmer called Tama Shanta,' said Jerry.

He carried on talking about Tama going home after drinking and heard bagpipes. He followed the music to a graveyard. Jerry then described a scene, quite lovely, but spine shivering.

The devil playing the instrument was in the middle surrounded by boys sitting in coffins holding candles with witches dancing in circles. One called Nana was very beautiful wearing just a short shirt called a cutty sark. Soon Nana began to dance very well.

'Well done to the one in the Cutty Sark!' cried Tama.

The witches began chasing him. Witches can't cross water so Tama got on a horse and headed for a nearby stream. Nana reached out to stop him. She only caught the horses tail and Tama crossed the stream.

'The builder of the ship took the picture of Nana and the horse tail and made the front piece of Nana holding the horse tail. He called the ship Cutty Sark after Nana's clothing,' exclaimed Jerry.

Then we heard about Franklin and the Arctic. I'm just going to say they got lost, had lead poisoning, became cannabals then died and nobody heard what happened to Bullot's rescue search.

A statue has been put up in memory of Bullot's golden heart and determination to find Franklin. I'm not going to tell the rest because it was horrible and I've seen photos of Franklin's feet to make it 100 per cent horrid.

My favourite bit was about Ann Boleyn and Henry VIII because I'm doing Tudors at school. Ann was watching a *jousting contest in which Henry was taking part. She dropped her handkerchief and a nobleman picked it up for her. Henry VIII noticed it. He put Ann Boleyn, this nobleman and three others guilty for plotting against the king to death.*

He made sure they were found guilty. They were sentenced to hang, drawn and quartered but Henry said that Ann was just a lady, so cut her head off.

The noblemen were hung till they were half-dead, had the stomach pulled out and cut into four. Ann had her head chopped off. The last place Ann saw the sky was at the jousting contest so they say that with her head tucked under her arm she goes to the place and looks at the sky when the midnight hour comes."

Evenings

Evenings out might need more planning. There are plenty of restaurants. One fun place to look out for is the **Clarendon Hotel** in Blackheath with its variety of theme nights.

Woolwich, Greenwich and The Dome have cinemas while **Greenwich Theatre**, **Princess of Orange Theatre** (Greenwich) and **Bob Hope Theatre** (Eltham) stage plays.

Blackheath Concert Halls put on a variety of musical performances and the occasional theatrical performance. **Greenwich Dance Agency** has the occasional dance performance. Older children might well want to see the live musical performances in the pubs of Greenwich and Blackheath.

Gay Greenwich

Greenwich is a relaxed area of London and has several venues popular with gays and lesbians including the **Rose and Crown** and **Gloucester pubs**. The **Albany** has a monthly gay club night. For more details contact the **Lesbian and Gay Officer** at **Greenwich Borough Offices.**

Ethnic Greenwich

Despite its maritime history Greenwich has a relatively small ethnic population. The exception is Thamesmead, which houses a 10,000 strong Vietnamese community originating in the aftermath of the Vietnamese War.

The borough had a small number of black people living in the area for centuries. Many black sailors served on Royal Navy ships and some black sailors stayed as retired pensioners at the Seamen's Home, now the Royal Naval College.

Much of the area's wealth was based on the slave trade. St Alfege records the presence of a black servant in the home of a Virginia planter as early as 1699. The slave trade with all its horrors flourished under Elizabeth I who was aided by other faces familiar in Greenwich, Sir John Hawkins and his cousin, Sir Francis Drake. By 1704 Ambrose Crowley, who had built the Jacobean Crowley House in Highridge, Greenwich, had moved his premises to Greenwich. His London premises were too small for his trade – supplying the firm of Thomas Hall with manacles, ankle irons and collars for slave ships.

In the 18th century, 20 shipping merchants had their homes on Blackheath. Many of these were involved in the slave trade. William Innes of Grotes Place was a successful merchant in the Caribbean and campaigned against the abolition of slavery. John Julius Angerstein of Woodlands had a third share of a slave estate in Grenada. Thomas King who lived in Dartmouth Grove was a partner in the notorious slave agents firm, Camden, Calvert and King while Duncan Campbell, Overseer of the Prison Hulks, lived in Orchard House and owned a plantation in Jamaica.

Brigadier Hunter of Charlton was Governor of Jamaica in 1734. He had many black slaves in his Charlton home. Sir William Langhorne whose ghost is still said to haunt his last home, Charlton House, was Governor of Madras in 1670 at the time of the wars with the Indian peoples.

Despite Elizabeth having banned black people from Britain, the black and Asian population remained and grew. Many blacks in the borough had won their freedom and there are suggestions of a small community developing in Woolwich, which was a centre for the reselling of slaves. One former slave who became famous in Greenwich was Ignatius Sancho; the first black African writer living in Britain to have his work published in the country.

Ignatius's mother died giving birth to him on a slave ship in 1729. His father was one of the many slaves who had thrown themselves overboard rather than endure the misery of slavery. At two, Ignatius was lodged with three sisters in Greenwich. Teaching himself to read and write, he eventually found support from the Duke and Duchess of Montague at Montague House in Blackheath. The duke lent him books and then employed Ignatius as his butler. So renowned was Ignatius as a playwright, poet and composer that **Gainsborough** painted his portrait.

Other famous blacks include Olaudah Equiano, a former slave who lived at 111 Maze Hill and published his autobiography in 1789. Equiano joined John Julius Angerstein's Committee of the Black Poor that raised funds for blacks and their families to settle in a new free life back in Africa, in Sierra Leone. Three ships eventually set sail. On board were also 74 white women, many of who were married to black men. Unable to stomach the possibility of inter-racial marriage, many in society circles suggested that the women were prostitutes or had been coerced into the journey.

Dr George Rice was a black American who studied under Joseph Lister at Edinburgh University. He moved to Plumstead and became Medical Superintendent of the **Woolwich Workhouse Infirmary** in 1881.

INTRODUCTION

Eltham's St John the Baptist Church has a headstone recording the death in 1794 of Yemmerawanyea Kebbarah. He and Bennelong were the first native Australians (Aborigines) to set foot in England. Yemmerawanyea died in Eltham at 19 having spent just one year in the country. Bennelong returned to Sydney where a district is named after him.

Today there is still only a small black and Asian community. The two **Sikh temples** and a mosque in Woolwich give evidence of the Asian community's presence. Many Asians and North Africans have settled around the mosque as shown by the number of halal Indian takeaways at the Woolwich end of Plumstead High St.

Woolwich also has a **synagogue**. The **Greenwich Chinese Association** has a community school near Maze Hill (tel 0208 858 2410) offering advice and education. Greenwich Borough Museum in Plumstead has an ethnic minorities section. **Afro-Caribbeans** in Greenwich are pressing for an Afro-Caribbean Heritage Centre. The *Paradise Bar* reggae club is the only club dedicated to Afro-Caribbean music.

Getting There

Greenwich's nearest **airport** is *London City Airport* in the Royal Docks on the north side of the river close to the *Woolwich Ferry*. A train from Prince Regent station on the *Docklands Light Railway (DLR)* line links with the new Jubilee line to the Cutty Sark. The DLR operates fully automated, driverless trains on an elevated track offering excellent views of the docks and the city.

Flying to London's *Heathrow Airport* requires a rail trip into the heart of the city to reach *Bank* tube station and taking the DLR or travelling to *Waterloo* to take the *Jubilee Line* to *North Greenwich* tube station. *London Gatwick Airport* requires taking an overhead line to *London Bridge* or *Victoria*.

In the north of Greenwich Borough there are five overland **rail stations** on the same line. They are *Greenwich* on Greenwich High Rd, *Maze Hill* which is on the east side of Greenwich Royal Park and a short walk from the National Maritime Museum, *Westcombe Park* on Westcombe Hill, *Charlton* on Charlton Church Lane, close to the Thames Barrier, and *Woolwich Dockyard.* Trains from London to Greenwich depart from *Charing Cross, Waterloo* and *London Bridge* stations every 15 to 30 minutes taking around 17 minutes.

In the south of the borough trains pass through *Blackheath station* in Blackheath Village, *Kidbrooke* on Kidbrooke Park Road, *Eltham* on Well Hall Road and *Falconwood* beside Rochester Way.

On the **London Underground**, the *Jubilee Line* with a stop at *North Greenwich* for the *Dome*, connects Greenwich with *Stratford* and *Lewisham* and links up with *Charing Cross, Waterloo* and *London Bridge*. At last, the new line has put Greenwich on the tube route around London.

The stylish way to arrive in Greenwich is on the Thames by **boat**. *River Trip Line* (tel 0839 1213432) run boat trips to Greenwich and the *Thames Barrier* in Charlton from *Westminster, Charing Cross* and *Tower* piers. *Catamaran Cruisers* (0207 987 1185) sail to Greenwich from Charing Cross and Tower Piers.

Tidal Cruises (0207 930 3373) sail to the *Thames Barrier* from *Westminster Pier* between March and November and *Westminster Passenger Service Association* (0207 930 4097) run a half-hourly service to Greenwich from Westminster.

For those who would rather travel to Greenwich on a London **bus,** number 188 operated by Arriva, goes to the *Cutty Sark* in Greenwich from *Elephant & Castle, Waterloo, Holborn, Russell Square* and *Euston* tube stations (peak times every 10 minutes, off peak 12-20 minutes). *Bus 53* operated by Stagecoach goes to *Blackheath, Charlton, Woolwich* and *Plumstead* from *New Cross Gate, Elephant & Castle, Lambeth North, Westminster, Trafalgar Square, Piccadilly* and *Oxford Circus* tube stations (peak times every 10 minutes, off peak 12-15 minutes).

Bus X53 operated by Stagecoach in peak hours on weekdays only goes to *Blackheath, Charlton, Woolwich* and *Thamesmead* from *New Cross, New Cross Gate, Elephant & Castle, Westminster, Trafalgar Square, Piccadilly* and *Oxford Circus* tube stations (every 20 minutes).

Bus 321 operated by London Central goes to *Eltham* from *New Cross Gate* tube station (peak time every 8 minutes, off peak 15-20 minutes).

Travellers on the tubes, buses and local trains can make their trips much cheaper by buying a range of daily, weekly and monthly **travel cards** which allow for transport on all three services across the length and breadth of London. Details are available from ticket offices. For **24 hour travel information** telephone 0207 222 1234, for **free local guides** and timetables phone 0207 371 0247.

For those travelling by **car,** the **A2 road** links Greenwich with the **M25 Motorway** which circles London, joining up with the M11, M1, M40, M4, M5 and M23 motorways, and the A12, A1, and A3 (see diagrams). The **A200** and A2 link Greenwich with *Central London* south of the Thames. *Woolwich Free Ferry* on the *A206* takes cars across to the north side of the Thames to reach M11. The *Blackwall Tunnel (A102M)* passes beneath the *Millennium Dome* for central London north of the Thames and the *M11.*

Getting Around within Greenwich

Cycling is an eco-friendly way of getting around the district and The *Original Bike Hire Company* (tel 0208 691 5317) rent out bicycles from *Greenwich Pier.* The **rail** service between Greenwich and *Abbey Wood* is very regular and efficient, while the **bus** services are plentiful and cover all parts of the borough. During the Millennium celebrations **parking** will be difficult anywhere near the Dome. Taking public transport is a wiser option. *Bus 108* links the *Dome* with *Blackheath, Greenwich,* and *Charlton. Bus 477* links the Dome with *Woolwich* and *Plumstead.*

The key road in the borough for those travelling by **car** is the **A206**, which, from west to east, links up with the **A102M** to the **Dome (Blackwall Tunnel)**, **Charlton** (Thames Barrier), **Woolwich** (Free Ferry), **Plumstead** and **Thamesmead**. The **A2** links **Blackheath** with **Eltham**. After Blackheath the A2 which followed the Roman Watling Rd to **Dover** shifts south while the continuation of the Watling Rd is the **A207** which passes over **Shooters Hill.**

Woolwich is linked to **Eltham** by the **A205**. The passenger ferry, which sails from Greenwich to the Thames Barrier, is a handy way to get to Charlton.

Tourist Information

Greenwich Tourist Information Office is moving from its site on Greenwich Church St but more details can be found at the Greenwich Pier site. **London Tourist Board Visitor Call** (tel. 0839 123456) service costs callers 49 pence per minute.

"Council street cleaners in Greenwich are being given training to help them cope with queries from tourists." - The *Guardian* Newspaper July 14th, 1999.

Tour guides are available on almost any subject from Greenwich Pier ticket office or by telephoning **Greenwich Tour Guide Association** (tel. 0208 858 6169).

Communications

Telephoning Britain requires putting the numbers 0044 before the local code so that 0208 345 6789 becomes 0044 181 345 6789. London is also changing the prefix to its numbers so that 0181 becomes 0208 and 0044 181 345 6789 becomes 0044208 345 6789 etc. 0171 numbers have become 0207 numbers.

Sending **letters** to Europe currently costs a minimum of 34 pence and elsewhere 44 pence. The British postal service is still one of the most efficient in the world for sending letters. For parcels there are plenty of options in the **Yellow Pages** phone directories. **Post offices** will take parcels and packages for sending off and are found in each of the borough's districts.

Remember, Greenwich time is **Greenwich Mean Time (GMT)** but clocks go forward by one hour at the end of March to **British Summer Time (BST)** and go back by one hour, reverting to GMT at the end of October.

Other Helpful Numbers

Greenwich Tourist Information: 0208 858 6376

Greenwich Leisure Service: 0208 854 8888

Emergency Services, Ambulance, Police and Fire Brigade: 999

Greenwich District Hospital: 0208 858 8141

GREENWICH TOWN

Greenwich Town Centre

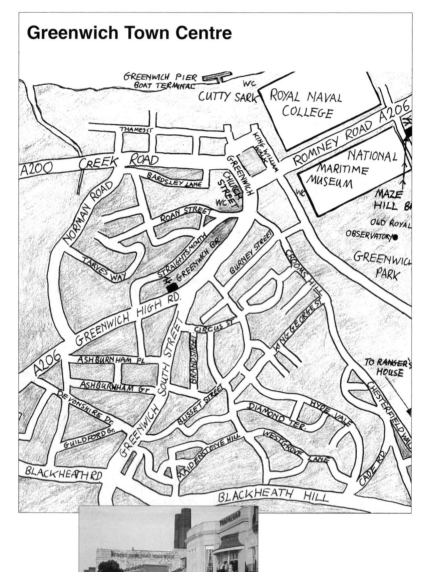

REGAL **Greenwich Town**

Sat right on the banks of a loop of the Thames, Greenwich town recounts in its buildings and exhibitions the story of a millennium of regal and maritime history; the story of England. By the country's main river, just outside the country's capital and on the main road to the European continent, the town's location gave it exceptional importance.

Greenwich grew up on the edge of Kent which was populated by Celts, then Jutes from Denmark and Holland. In AD43 Roman Emperor Claudius sent 40,000 troops to control the British Isles. Their capital, Londinum, grew and Greenwich developed as a small port and stop off point on the Watling Rd. When the Romans left Britain in 405AD, London went into decline.

By the 11th century Viking longship raiders were targeting London and the Thames estuary. 50 longships at a time would be moored at Greenwich while the Vikings pursued their plunderous raids. The Vikings were so confident that they would moor all winter at Greenwich.

During the 9th century Greenwich was ruled by King Alfred the Great, the king who burnt the cakes. It was already a busy port and Alfred gave the district to his daughter Elstrudis. Her husband, Baldwin II, the Count of Flanders died in 918 and some historians say that she then made gifts of the Manors of Lewisham, Greenwich and Woolwich to St Peter's Abbey of Ghent in Flanders.

King Edgar, "Emperor of England" is also credited by some with granting the Manors to the Flemish friars in 964. Either way it proved a troublesome gift which by 1012 would draw King Ethelred into a battle with the Vikings. In that year the Vikings moored again at Greenwich for their winter stay.

The Viking raids ventured far inland and they laid siege to Canterbury. After 20 days the city surrendered. The buildings were sacked and many people slaughtered. The subsequent killing of the Archbishop of Canterbury provoked a war. Thurkill the Viking commander of a fleet of 45 longships was said to be so disapproving of the murder of the archbishop, Alfege, that he switched sides joining King Ethelred's forces. However, Ethelred was defeated and Thurkill fled with the king to Normandy.

The Manor of Lewisham remained in the hands of the Flemish. Resentment grew at the people's taxes being sent abroad. In 1400 during the One Hundred Years' War with France, King Edward III declared that the Manor could not be kept in the hands of people who might have sympathy with the French. Henry V confiscated the land in 1414 when he passed a bill expropriating, "alien houses" and in the 1420s the Manor was given to his youngest brother, Humphrey, Duke of Gloucester.

On his brother's death which left a young child of 12 as heir, the Duke of Gloucester, became the Lord Protector of England. In this powerful position the Duke began to build his palace, Bella Court in Greenwich. In 1433 Parliament granted the Duke the right to enclose a park of 200 acres for hunting purposes. He died the victim of a royal plot and the Manor became the property of the Queen, Margaret of Anjou. The Queen had been based at Eltham Palace and sent Kettlewell to refurbish and beautify Bella Court.

Henry VI died in the tower at the hands of Edward IV. The new palace also attracted the next queen, Edward IV's wife, Elisabeth Woodville, who came from the Manor of Lee next door. The Palace of Placentia was born. However it was Henry VII who is credited with building Placentia to its magnificence at the beginning of the 1500s.

Henry VIII was born in the palace in 1491. Placentia and Eltham were Henry VIII's favourite palaces until he moved to Hampton Court, further up river. He would travel from Westminster by barge and hold many wild parties and banquets in its halls. In 1522 at Placentia Henry's three year old sister, Queen Mary, was married to the Dauphin of France. Present was French Bourbon **Emperor Charles V**. One musician attached to the Royal Chapel was Tudor composer and father of English church music, **Thomas Tallis**.

From Placentia Henry plotted the downfall of his first queen Katharine of Aragon. Subsequently he ordered that several local friars be slaughtered and began in earnest the process known as the Dissolution of the Monasteries, destroying the power base of his enemies in the Catholic Church.

Jousting contests held in the palace's tiltyard were the king's favourite sporting events and Shooters Hill was the scene of many pageants participated in by the king and his queens. It was at one of the jousting tournaments that his queen Anne Boleyn is said to have dropped her handkerchief, enticing four knights to pick it up. The queen was accused of unfaithfulness and was subsequently executed along with the knights.

Near Greenwich stood the Mansion of the Old Court, home to the Duke of Northumberland. Legend has it that the young king, **Edward VI**, was on his death bed, kept alive with doses of arsenic by the duke. The duke was plotting to put **Lady Jane Grey** on the throne and needed to prevent a succession until his plans were in place. Edward died and Lady Jane became queen.

The coup sparked an uprising led by Thomas Wyatt and Lady Jane was ousted after ten days. The unfortunate queen was executed along with her family and the Duke of Northumberland. **Mary I** took the throne to be followed by her sister, **Queen Elizabeth I** who was also born at Placentia. Charles I used the palace and later built what is now known as **Queen's House** for his wife in the nearby palace grounds, later renamed **Greenwich Royal Park**.

When **Oliver Cromwell** came to power at the time of the Commonwealth, Placentia was badly damaged and stripped for timber. Charles II had plans to build a new palace on the spot but was thwarted through lack of funds. Only the Tudor crypt of Placentia's Great Hall remains. This undercroft is beneath the west range of the Queen Anne block of the Royal Naval College. It has been cut into three chambers by the foundation walls of the Queen Anne block.

The tale of royal history of Greenwich then switched to Queen's House and the magnificent **Seamen's Hospital** built on the site where Placentia stood. Both these buildings still stand today as two of the great architectural heritages of England.

The Royal Naval College

Still Navy property, our access into the college grounds from King William Walk required meeting the security police. The **Royal Naval College** (which until 1869 was known as the Royal Hospital for Seamen) was built as a charity home for retired and disabled seamen. With the Restoration following Cromwell's rule **Charles II** assumed the throne and requested that **Christopher Wren** build a riverside palace. What is now known as the Charles block, and soon to house the Trinity College of Music, was the original royal palace of Charles II. However, it was never completed due to lack of funds and never occupied by the king.

In 1677, Queen Mary II married William of Orange in a political marriage that secured a Protestant alliance against Catholic France. England, at war with France, defeated the old enemy in the decisive battle of La Hogue. The Nine Year War rumbled on in Europe for some time but the battle ensured that the Catholic, James II, would not return to the throne.

By then, Greenwich had built up a great sea-faring tradition as home to the fleet moored close by Deptford and Woolwich Royal Dockyards. It was in Greenwich that Sir Walter Raleigh, that great English marine adventurer, is said to have thrown his cloak down for Queen Elizabeth I to walk on and thus avoid muddying her shoes.

Mary II wanted to build the Royal Hospital for Seamen for old sailors as a twin to the Chelsea hospital for soldiers. She commissioned the building of what is now called the Royal Naval College. She felt that the old sailors would feel more at home by the river which they had sailed so often when travelling to and from the English Channel. Near the top of the building one can see the balconies from which they could gaze out onto the great river.

Originally the architect of the building was to be John Webb but he only com-

Queen's House, Greenwich

pleted the east section of the King Charles block. Work was carried on to a new design by Christopher Wren who was aided by **Nicholas Hawksmoor** and **John Vanbrugh**, among the most influential architects of their day. The building was completed in 1696 by which time Mary II was dead and William III on the throne alone.

When the Seamen's Hospital (on King William Walk and close to the Cutty Sark) was built, Christopher Wren wanted one building with a great dome similar to St Pauls Cathedral which he had also designed. However, Queen Mary had insisted that the seamen's hospital should not obscure her view from **Queen's House**. To accommodate her wishes Wren opted to split the hospital into the four dramatically symmetrical buildings which exist today and between which one can view the Thames from Queen's House. The west front and east range of the King William block are more baroque in style, and so individual that they are considered to be the work of Hawksmoor.

We climbed the steps and went in to view the magnificent **Painted Hall** and the splendid 18th century art work of **Sir James Thornhill**. We stood with our backs to the entrance hall to view the magnificent arcade with columns passing over to the east wing and the Chapel.

The grandiose hall with its size and depth is quite stunning. The style, English Baroque, lasted for only 30 years. A fire in the chapel 20 years later destroyed the interior, also in English Baroque. The Age of Reason was storming England and the style in the chapel was changed to the roccoco of James 'Athenian' Stuart.

The Painted Hall was conceived as a magnificent dining hall for the old matelots. Long tables and chairs are laid out as if expecting the old sea dogs to arrive at any moment. The windows gave them a view of the Thames and the dome of the east wing.

The interior decorations were made by the English baroque architect, **Nicholas Hawksmoor** and the paintings by **Sir James Thornhill**. Thornhill began his work in 1707 and completed it in 1727. He painted the dry plaster ceilings in oil and the 45ft high walls in monochrome. The room is remarkable for the liberal use of monochrome, the painted pilasters, the gilt Corinthian capitals and gilt corniche.

The hall ceiling is entirely painted covering an area 160ft by 51ft. The centre oval is a historic painting in *trompe l'oeil* style portraying a window to the heavens. Its theme is the Apotheosis, the ascension to heaven of William III and Mary II at the centre of the picture. Part history, part allegory, part mythology it is called the triumph of peace and liberty over tyranny.

The Protestant alliance of William and Mary signifies peace and liberty while tyranny is portrayed as King Louis XIV of France. William with his right hand receives an olive branch from Concorde who is shown as having the lamb and the doves. With his left hand William passes the Athenian cap of liberty to Europe signified by the white horse.

Beneath their feet Father Time bears up the figure of Naked Truth. To his left are drawings of the seamen's home. Beneath them are Hercules carrying a huge club and Minerva with a spear as Truth driving the demons from heaven.

The picture is also said to be an allegory of time, a major theme of maritime Greenwich. At the top above the royal canopy is Apollo, the source of light, driving the sun across the heavens and sprinkling the hours on his way. Around the interior of the oval are the signs of the zodiac starting from Aries through to Pisces. The four seasons are portrayed. The old man with the grey beard was painted by Thornhill using a naval pensioner called John Wall as a model. Wall was 97 years old and still often in trouble for drunkenness and causing a nuisance.

At the end of the oval is a British Man of War, the Blenheim of 1740, loaded with treasure taken from a Spanish galleon above William's head with its gun ports open.

Mary died before the decoration of the building began. William III died without any heirs and Queen Anne, Mary's younger sister, ascended the throne. The ceiling of the upper hall is devoted to Queen Anne and her consort, Prince George of Denmark, who was the Lord High Admiral. Both liked a bit of a tipple and this is portrayed in the painting. Anne had seventeen pregnancies but only five children lived of which only one reached the age of eleven.

Anne died and the succession went through the granddaughter of James I, whose son, George I, began the house of Hanover. The end wall therefore has a portrait of the Hanoverian family, and is meant to illustrate the importance and continuity of the House of Hanover. The Hanoverians held the throne for 187 years from 1714 until Queen Victoria died in 1901.

As we left we paid attention to the Gothic height of the entrance hall rising 60ft and topped with a cupola. Look up and you will see the four winds depicted in the cupola. You will also see listed all the contributors to the construction of the hall. The walls record William III donating £19,500, the Archbishop of Canterbury, £200, and Queen Anne £6,472.

A lift and steps took us down to the basement to the old officers' coffee shop. At the last major function the officers pulled down the white ensign which now hangs in the chapel. The officers would have to dine here in uniform but they can relax today. Now the coffee shop is known as the **Old Royal Naval College Coffee Shop** which opened to the public in 1999. This spacious shop is superbly decorated and well laid out. It was the **Queen Elizabeth Ante Room** and displays a large picture of the Queen.

The food was delicious particularly the home made cakes at £1.50 and the varied Piazza D'Oro coffees at £1.25, first class. A savoury course cost £4.50. I tried the coconut meringue with a jam filling. Service is to officer standard and by silver trolley service, it is delivered by the former staff of the officers' coffee house. The shop is licensed, with wine at £4.50 a bottle and beer available. Retired servicemen still drop in for coffee and are known as the Wednesday Club for their weekly attendance. The coffee house is not well known, so we decided it was worth a return visit to sample a slice of elegant unhurried style.

Until recently, the building (0181 858 2154) was a working college for the Royal Navy. Today it is open to the public. The Painted Hall which seats 375 people is available for Sunday dinners and private functions (around £4,000).

Opening times are daily between noon and 5pm when the Painted Hall is open. Disability access is by prior arrangement with the college management or approaching the Yeoman on the door.

Sketches lined the walls of the building, illustrating the history of Placentia, the College and Greenwich. We took an underground passage known as the Chalk Walk to the east wing and the old officers' bar. The series of arches and a vaulted ceiling were added to by the display of officers' crests. The walkway led to a skittle alley where indentations on the side of the windows were created by notches believed to have been made by the matelots.

We arrived at the Queen Mary building with pictures illustrating how the west dining room appeared in 1860. The bar is quite superb with its columns. The coal fireplace and arched benches and bar make it a very homely drinking den, and is now available for functions.

The Chalk Walk emerged into the porch of the building's other showpiece, **The Chapel**. As we entered the organist was playing above the entry adding life and meaning to this ancient place of maritime worship. As we entered on our right stood a bas relief depicting the loss of the British ship, Orpheus, off the coast of New Zealand in 1873 when 166 officers, seamen and marines lost their lives.

Horatio Nelson, King of the Fleet

Horatio Nelson was probably Britain's greatest ever commander of the fleet. His naval exploits in claiming the seas for the British crown against the revolutionary forces of France, Italy and Spain have for two centuries been told to every child in the land. His greatest victory came with his death at Cadiz in the Battle of Trafalgar.

In October 1797 Nelson lost his arm in a battle. He stayed at Greenwich as a guest of the Lieutenant Governor of the Seamen's Home. When he died in 1805 at Trafalgar his body was brought back pickled. Later he was put in a coffin made from the firwood which had been the mast of the French ship, L'Orient blown up in the Battle of the Nile. The firwood was then surrounded by lead and British oak.

News of Nelson's death had just reached the celebrating English when a hand picked crew of his best men on HMS Victory moored in the Thames. It was a stormy Xmas Eve when his body was taken to the Upper Hall of the Seamen's home. The country had fallen into mourning. Nelson's body lay in state in the Painted Hall.

In January of the new year Nelson's body was taken for burial to Westminster down the Thames in a procession of barges. At their head were 500 pensioners who had served with their hero. His companion at sea, Thomas Hardy was subsequently promoted to Sea Lord, made a baron and Governor of the Seamen's Hospital. His surgeon on the Victory, Dr Beattie, became the home's doctor wearing the bullet he had extracted from Nelson as a brooch.

Nearby stood a marble bust of Sir Thomas Hardy, companion in arms of Horatio Nelson. Once Governor of Greenwich Hospital, Hardy died in 1839

The first chapel was completed in 1752 by Ripley to the designs of Wren. In English Baroque style, it was a plainer chapel with less ornate galleries than seen today. The emphasis was on space and proportion rather than embellishment. Fire gutted the chapel in 1779. The current chapel, a Georgian period peace, was finally completed to the design of James 'Athenian' Stuart in 1789.

Stuart had made an extensive study of Greek classical architecture and used what became known as the roccoco style with Ionic columns, fluted pilasters and many ornamentations in plaster reflecting Greek styles.

At 45ft, the height of the ceiling is the same as that of the Painted Hall though the chapel's ceiling is curved producing excellent accoustics for the Baroque organ, one of the country's largest and best preserved.

A 25ft by 14ft picture, the work of American-born **Benjamin West**, portrays the preservation of St Paul as recorded in the Bible. The gilt frame around the picture is the product of a local wood carver.

The altar is a slab of marble supported by six cherubim with the use of coade-stone made in Lambeth. Just beneath the ceiling tromp l'oeil and monochrome are brought into use with pictures of the saints and chiaroscuro paintings of the Apostles and Evangelists and the Ascension of Christ by the artist Rebecca. The decorations around the lower windows on copper plates are also in *chiaroscuro*, portraying scenes from the life of Christ.

The 12ft high sky blue marble architrave, cornice and frieze in the interior portal were carved in one piece by the court sculptor, **John Bacon**.

The floor is in veined marble producing a rope design. The ceiling had huge chandeliers which had to be winched up with lighted candles. As in the Painted Hall, the room was heated by fire and the ceiling displays the former chimney holes allowing smoke to escape.

The College Chapel (for the verger tel 0208 858 2380) is open to the public and still holds a weekly Sunday service where visitors are invited to take Holy Communion.

Nearby is the old **Dreadnought Seamen's Hospital**. As we passed it was being transformed into a residence for Greenwich University students.

Queen's House

An aerial view of the north end of Greenwich Royal Park illustrates a glorious symmetry imposed by the designers of this classic corner of British history. Down the centre of the park lies the pathway to Blackheath leading to the statue of **General James Wolfe** on the hill which sweeps down to Queen's House. On each side of the house are the gleaming white colonnades that stretch to the **National Maritime Museum**. Another path leads from the front of Queen's House bounded by the magnificent buildings of the Royal Naval College looking out on the Thames.

At the heart is the fabulous **Queen's House** (tel 0208 858 4422). The first building in Britain totally reflecting the classic revival, it was designed in 1616 by **Inigo Jones** one of Britain's most famous architects. The white villa was commissioned by James I for his consort Queen Anne but later given by Charles I to his French wife, Henrietta Maria, in 1635. Forced to flee during the Civil War and the rule of Oliver Cromwell, the widow queen returned in 1660 with the Restoration, as Dowager to her son, Charles II. In 1662 **John Webb** enlarged the house.

The house was also used by Charles II. Oliver Cromwell ordered the house to be sold but having secured a purchaser, the Puritan leader changed his mind and left the house as government property. When Charles II took the throne he wanted to rebuild the palace by the river but with coffers empty the project failed.

The Queen's House was built as two wings united by a bridge crossing the old Deptford to Woolwich Rd. Later John Webb added two

General James Wolfe

more bridges allowing the house to become a unified whole under which runs an arch for the cobbled carriageway. The road was switched away from the house to what is now Romney Rd.

The house has been restored and houses a collection of court and marine paintings. In the 1920s a couple believed that they had seen a ghost on the stairs of the house. However, examination of a photograph which they took at the time proved inconclusive.

Inigo Jones was inspired by the work of Italian architect, **Palladio**. The ground floor is of rusticated stone and the upper floors are brick with a delicate if restrained design. From the park one gets a view of the villa's fine recessed loggia supported by Ionic columns and the symmetrical placing of the windows.

Going inside one enters the Great Hall, a perfect cube with a chess board marble floor by sculptor **Nicholas Stone** which matches the design of the ceiling's carved wooden beams by Inigo Jones. A cantilevered staircase, where the ghosts are said to have been seen, spirals up to the first floor. It is known as the Tulip Staircase because of the design of the wrought iron bannister.

Up the stairs are the magnificent King's and Queen's Apartments. The King's Apartments include a Presence Chamber, an Anteroom, a Privy Chamber, an Antechamber and a Bedchamber. The Queen's Apartment has a similar collection of rooms plus the Queen's Closet. The rooms include dramatic plasterwork, beamed ceilings and elegant friezes and fireplaces. In the Queen's Presence Chamber there are lovely murals and panels decorated by fantasy figures, royal emblems and exotic designs. While some of the work is 19th century or later, most of it is original 17th century work.

The east and west wings of the house are the beautiful white colonnades. Added by Daniel Alexander between 1807 and 1816, they emphasise the unity of the whole complex. Queen's House is due to re-open after refurbishment for the Millennium celebrations.

National Maritime Museum

We entered the rest of National Maritime Museum which today lays claim to being the world's largest maritime museum. It houses 4,000 oil paintings, 50,000 prints and drawings, 3,000 ship models, 70 boats, 1,300 scientific instruments, 100,000 books, 750,000 ship plans, 50,000 charts, 250,000 photo negatives, manuscripts and shelving stretching for two miles.

Apart from that it is a magnificent building worth a visit in its own right. The New Wing was added in 1862 by Phillip Hardwick and the Neptune Hall, once a gymnasium was added in 1873. Like the South West Wing added in 1876, these extensions all compliment the classical style of Queen's House.

The current displays are split across three floors. A tour takes roughly one hour, assuming one doesn't linger too much. We found it all quite magnificent, mixing British and international maritime history, the modern and the new, record breaking speedboats, barges, yachts and the rudders from ocean liners. The whole central area is covered by a 2,500 square metre free-span glass roof, the largest of its kind in Europe.

Entering level 1 we came across the gold leafed 18th century barge of Prince Frederick used by George III. Even the tiller was covered in gold leaf. Opposite hung the huge stern of the 74-gun HMS Implacable which fought alongside Nelson's HMS Victory at the Battle of Trafalgar.

Passing down the right of the hall was the yacht used by **Robin Knox-Johnston** to win the round the world boat race in 1968, so becoming the first yachtsmen to navigate the world non-stop. I remember the tragic storey of one of the competitors, **Donald Crowhurst**, and found it revealed in the chilling but beautiful, *Teignmouth Electron* work of artist **Tacita Dean** on Level 2.

Crowhurst disappeared sailing through the Caribbean. Reading extracts from

National Maritime Museum

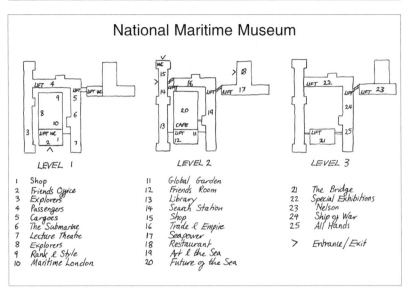

LEVEL 1

1 Shop
2 Friends Office
3 Explorers
4 Passengers
5 Cargoes
6 The Submarine
7 Lecture Theatre
8 Explorers
9 Rank & Style
10 Maritime London

LEVEL 2

11 Global Garden
12 Friends Room
13 Library
14 Search Station
15 Shop
16 Trade & Empire
17 Seapower
18 Restaurant
19 Art & the Sea
20 Future of the Sea

LEVEL 3

21 The Bridge
22 Special Exhibitions
23 Nelson
24 Ship of War
25 All Hands

> Entrance/Exit

his diaries it appeared that the harsh experience had driven him insane. His boat, *Teignmouth Electron,* was found washed up in the Cayman Islands. Crowhurst was never seen again. One French competitor had a different experience. Reaching the finishing line, he couldn't stop and ended up going round the world one and a half times over!

On Level 1, we came across another eerie tale of yore in an atmospheric gallery painted ice-white with a whistling wind emanating from the public address system. It was the gallery revealing the nightmarish story of the 19th century explorer, Franklin's attempt to discover the North West Passage through the waters and ice flows of North America.

There in a cavern were displayed his boot and the tin cans from which he is believed to have contracted lead poisoning. Some of the bones found of men who died on the expedition showed scratch marks. These marks, it is suggested, were consistent with cannibalism. Did they eat their compatriots?

On level 2 our attention was grabbed by the display of old naval uniforms including that of the five year old Prince Albert. The matelots uniforms were mounted on dummies and shielded by closet doors. We opened the doors and peered in not quite knowing if one of them might reveal a live model. Another gallery had displays on the British slave trade.

Level 3 revealed lots of interactive exhibits, mainly it must be said, for children. In the All Hands interactive gallery we found children sending each other morse signals, loading cargo and firing a gun at sea.

Next door in the Bridge Gallery an elderly couple were playing on the Viking boat, one steering and one rowing. Their task was to navigate sandbanks, driftwood and other obstacles to row their boat home. They failed and so did we, retiring for a cup of coffee in the Level 3 cafe. Great fun for the kids and all the family.

The Nelson Gallery is located on Level 3, with 500 exhibits relating to Nelson's sea battles and his private life, including the blood-stained uniform in which the national hero was killed at the Battle of Trafalgar, and Turner's controversial painting of the historic battle.

There's also a gallery on pollution, global warming and the oceans. The museum contains the vast **library**, a research area with ten computer screens, two **shops**, a **restaurant**, a **cafe** and has its own **web-site**, www.nmm.ac.uk. **Entry costs** are £7.50 for adults, £6 for concessions and children under 16 are free. Combined entry to the Old Royal Observatory costs are adults £9.50, concessions £7.60 with children free.

Opening hours are daily 10am-5pm, last entry 4.30pm (tel 0208 858 4422). Photography is prohibited as are smoking, eating and drinking in the galleries. Lecture and seminar facilities are available and the museum has an elegant function room for hire.

The museum has **wheelchair access** to all levels, parking for visitors with **disabilities** (make sure you book tel 0208 312 6730), and free large print and braille guides, audio-tape introductions, tactile plans and touch packs are available from the information desk (tel 0208 312 6608). Special tour guides can be booked by phoning 0208 312 6608.

Greenwich Royal Park

Greenwich Royal Park is the oldest of London's royal parks and one of my personal favorites with its ancient trees in tranquil surroundings and the escarpment offering panoramic views of London. The park was once attached to the **Palace of Placentia** by the river, home to the former palace hunting grounds, and was particularly enjoyed by Henry VIII and Elizabeth I. The formal landscape which one sees today was in its essence laid down in 1662 by Versailles gardener/designer Andre le Notre at the behest of Charles II who wanted a more Versailles type elegance.

The park, first bought by the Duke of Gloucester for Bella Court, was part of a vast hunting territory stretching from Epping to Eltham, filled with **deer** and wild boar for Henry VIII's gaming pleasures. James I walled the park and Charles II had the lake built and introduced more deer which are still in evidence in the park. Until 1906 they roamed free. In 1928 a man was killed in the park by a stag. Since then they have been kept in **The Wilderness** enclosure in the south east corner of the park. There are viewpoints to see the deer.

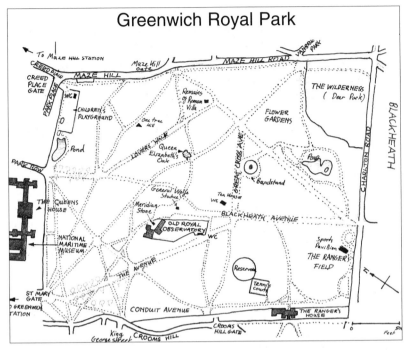

Greenwich Royal Park

Adjacent to the deer are flower gardens with flower beds, shrubs, some centuries old chestnut trees and a lake visited by a large number of water-birds. The south west end across the Blackheath entry has less formal rock gardens. Known as The Dell, it is populated with azaleas, camellia and rhododendron shrubs.

North east of Cafe Park House and slightly down the hill we came to a patch of huge old chestnut trees believed to have been planted in the 1670s. The ancient trees are now the foraging grounds for scores of grey squirrels who become especially busy when the trees shed their nuts in the autumn.

The leafy green park is an excellent place for a peaceful jog. The only exception is when it is used as the annual starting point for 30,000 runners taking part in the 26 mile long annual **London Marathon**.

Greenwich Observatory - The Meridian Line

The **Old Royal Observatory** (0208 858 4422) stands on the hill at the top of the park overlooking the Thames and Queen's House. We arrived from the Blackheath end avoiding the strenuous walk up the hill from Queen's House.

It was built as a navigational aid by Christopher Wren in 1676 at the instigation of Charles II. Charles was of the mind that as an astronomical observatory enabling study of the stars, it would contribute to what was considered the ancient and sole universal means of maritime navigation.

When Charles' interest waned, so did the finance and the building was constructed with recycled building materials and financed by the sale of what was said to have been faulty gunpowder.

The first Astronomer Royal was **John Flamsteed**. Wren himself a distinguished astronomer, designed the apartments. **The Octagon Room** is a rare interior design by Wren shaped to permit the astronomer to move about, check telescopes and time measurements.

Unpaid, Flamsteed had to rely on charity and fees from teaching students to survive. On his death his wife, Margaret, was forced sell all the Observatory's equipment and paintings. He was succeeded by **Edmund Halley**, a man of means. A member of the Royal Society, he was able to elevate appreciation of the post.

It was **Airy** who, as Astronomer Royal in the 18th century, established the Observatory as the **Prime Meridian** which was used by British ships for navigation.

In 1833 a red timeball was placed on top of the Observatory so that it could be seen by sailors on the Thames who used it to set their chronometers. It rose up the staff at 12.55 and fell regularly at 13.00 hours to indicate the time to sailors on the river and has done so (apart from a few lazy days) ever since.

In 1884, an international conference in Washington decided that Greenwich Mean Time, based on the line passing through the centre of the telescope of Airy's transit circle, would be the universal standard for the world. An imaginary line from Greenwich to the North and South Poles would be designated as 0 degrees longitude and all navigation and locations would henceforth report their distance from this line as so many degrees east or west.

The smoke from steam trains and increased factory pollution caused the Observatory to relocate to Herstmonceaux in Sussex. The building was damaged during the war but has been well restored. Today it houses Britain's largest refracting telescope. We climbed the steps entering the atmospheric dome where the huge 1.5 tonne, 28-inch telescope sat scanning the Universe.

Also on show are a fascinating and unique collection of historic timepieces and navigational instruments. Tele-scopes, astrolabes and sextants used to plot navigational charts and study the stars are just part of the important collection. Until 1837, Herschel's 40ft long telescope was the largest in the world. Now the remains are kept in a glass dome just in front of the **Planetarium** which is only open to the general public during school holidays.

Included are the clocks made by **Thomas Tompion**, 'father of English clock making' which Flamsteed used in his attempt to prove that the earth rotated at even time on its axis. Another is the H4 said to be the forerunner of precision watches and the H1 Clock designed by **John Harrison**, the scientist who won the prize offered in 1714 to solve the problem of measuring longitude. It's a fine place for kids and adults and hosts lots of children's activities, fun and games.

Entry to the Observatory **costs**; Adults £5, Concessions £4. Children go free.

(**Opening hours** are daily, 10am-5pm, last admission at 4.30pm, closed 24-26 Dec). There is level access to some parts but access to Flamsteed House requires negotiating four steps and other areas many more.

Royal Observatory, Greenwich

Outside on the Meridian line we saw the Accurist **Millenium Countdown Clock** which takes its position from the Global Positioning Satellite System, recording to one millionth of a second the time till the year 2,000.

Around the Park

We stood as so many others had stood by the grand statue of General James Wolfe, 150ft above the river and looking down on the plethora of fine Georgian terraces in Greenwich, before taking our opportunity to stand astride the meridian. With one foot in the Western Hemisphere and one foot in the Eastern Hemisphere, we found ourselves simultaneously ahead of and behind time. Now there's a riddle!

Soon after, we headed down the park road towards Blackheath and Rangers House and sat down for a cup of tea in the **Cafe Park House**. This attractive octagonal building has an upstairs function room with pleasant views of the park and provides good cheap basic food. It currently has a smoking area and outdoor tables.

Disability access is adequate (arrive from Blackheath) and the venue is popular for **children's parties**. Jazz musician, **Jools Holland**, is said to drop in from time to time and given the number of television and films in and around the park you may catch sight of stars from *The Bill* and *Brookside*.

Entering the west side of Greenwich Royal Park from Crooms Hill Road we came to a small red brick Roman-style building just above the path. This is **Conduit House** which was designed by Hawksmoor for carrying water to Queen's House. The underground pipes to the house are still present though no longer in use. Further up the hill is a sculpture by **Henry Moore**, *Standing Figure: Knife Edge,* erected in 1989. Nearby is a Saxon burial ground which was placed west of the Romano-British temple. Up the hill, close to the Vanbrugh Gate, are fragments of the raised floor of a Roman temple. The children's boating pool is also close to Park Vista and Queen's House.

Crooms Hill

Crums Hill is part of Greenwich Royal Park and from the junction with Greenwich High Road, close to St Alfege's church, we walked up the historic winding Crooms Hill road. This old street of the rich and the good flanks the west side of Greenwich Royal Park. At its foot is the **Village Market**, a small market place which we visited on a Sunday. On sale were new and second hand clothes, alternative jewellery, bric-a-brac in a busy market all given sustinence by a Thai stall selling very tasty hot food and tea.

Opposite is the very modern 82 bedroom **Ibis Hotel** (tel 0208 305 1177 fax 858 7139) at 30 Stockwell St. All its rooms are en suite with television, telephone and radio. Next door is the busy Cafe Rouge restaurant and coffee house.

Leaving the market we crossed the road and proceeded up the hill. To the small junction with Nevada Street. Quite narrow, Nevada Street was once known as Silver Street and part of the main road to Woolwich passing through the park and right through the archway beneath Queen's House. A statue of William IV, one of the borough's notable figures stands just before the park gates.

On the left towards the park is the **Old Coach Exchange.** A plaque on the wall notes that the building was once the stagecoach terminus with a booking office in the corner by the yard.

On the opposite corner is **Ye Olde Rose and Crown** pub. The site has been a place for drinking and entertainment since 1730 but the current building dates to the 1890s. Nowadays the **Rose and Crown** (0208 858 0154) sticks to serving ales, draught Becks, wines and a daily Sunday roast dinner. A sign in the window declares: "DOGS NEVER ALLOWED ON SUNDAYS. Other days allowed with landlord's permission". Sunday's a dry day for poor old Fido.

In 1855 the owners secured a music license, leading to the opening of Crowders Music Hall and, following several name changes, the **Greenwich Theatre.**

It's a favourite spot for famous actors to drop in. Rebuilt in 1969, the small theatre is popular for its intimacy. The theatre has a bar-cum-restaurant, Crowders, which is reported to have a great selection of food and friendly staff.

Climbing the hill, the 'Five Fair Houses' numbering 3 to 11, were built in 1702 to replace nine tenements given as annuity to Roan School in 1684 and securing an annual income of £6.

Crossing the road we faced a group of 17th and 18th century terraced houses. Being close to the Royal Park and away from central London's once crowded and dirty streets, this site was popular with nobles and worthies alike. A water pipe carries the initials of John Savary who built the block in 1721. A plaque at no.6 relates that former Poet Laureate, C. Day Lewis (father of film star Daniel Day Lewis) lived there between 1968 and 1973.

Number 12, Crooms Hill is actually two Georgian houses hosting the fascinating **Fan Museum**. It's the only one in the world devoted entirely to fans and fan crafting. It proved to be a fine educational exhibition. It may not be a well known museum but it's recommended for all those interested in high fashion and history and a must for the kids.

The Fan Museum

A brochure informed us that the museum houses the Helene Alexander collection of over 2,000 items which is to be given to the nation. Fan making has been taking place for centuries, especially to provide for the pleasure of the well-to-do around the world. Inside we would find on displays fans from Japan, China, France, England, Italy and numerours other countries. Many were decorated with fine paintings, while others were exquisitely carved in ivory, mother of pearl, tortoiseshell or wood. Some were gilt-edged or made using calf skin or lace.

Displayed in the entry on stretched calf skin was a magnificent fan presented in 1681 to the French Dauphin for his 20th birthday. Painted on the skin were his father King Louis XIV (of "L'etat c'est mois" fame) with his wife Queen Marie-Therese, the Duc D'Orleans, the Dauphin and his wife. The fans were notably closed as was the etiquette at court. Nearby were gilt-edged Italian fans made in 1750 and decorated with a reproduction of a Raphael painting.

Fans were so finely painted that it became fashionable after their use to break up the guard sticks. The gold was removed for recycling. The guard sticks were removed and the fan skins were stretched for mounting as panel pictures, several examples of which are exhibited.

Another room housed 17th century and some quite fantastic 18th century ivory fans. The interior has been restored to it's Georgian elegance and period furniture such as a Louis IX chair were also displayed giving the museum an air of the regal court. The museum offers viewers an audio-cassette and headphones to guide one round the exhibition. The 35 minute tape was extremely informative, giving details of not only the history and geography of fan crafting but also some humorous anecdotes.

The first floor is used for temporary exhibitions. At the time the Tsar's Exhibition had a marvellous display of fans, costumes, clothes, furniture and accessories from the Russian monarchy, including pieces from the notorious Catherine the Great and the ill-fated Tsar who met his death with the triumph of the epoch making Russian Revolution. Among the fans were little pocket fans, huge gold and silk wafters and others in ivory and satin. Of note were gloves, wallets lined with gold and golden snuff boxes.

Downstairs from the main entry we were invited to admire the Orangery of the listed town house. We were struck by the beautiful Japanese garden with its paved 18th century parterre, a stream and pond and, of course, fan-shaped flower beds. The Orangery has a splendidly decorated Georgian interior and is used as a cafeteria, making a good resting point before climbing the rest of Crooms Hill. Before we left we visited the shop on the ground floor with a range of fans, including Chinese, sandalwood and the current star, a £300 Millenium fan.

Entry to the Fan Museum (tel 0208 305 1441) costs £3.50 a head, £2.50 for concessions with free entry on Tuesdays between 2pm and 4.30pm for OAPs and those with disabilities. Groups are welcome as are enquiries about fans and their maintenance and the museum's monthly fan making classes (price £15). The class tutor, Caroline Allington is conservation adviser to the Historic Royal Palaces. The Orangery is available for weddings and other functions.

Opening hours, Tues-Sat 11am-4.30pm, Sunday noon-4.30pm, Mondays closed. Visiting hours are extended to 5pm during the summer.

Continuing up Crooms Hill we came to the houses of past courtiers and mayors on the right. On the left are the park railings. In 1830, the king wanted a high wall around his hunting reserve to keep out poachers and spies but the courtiers wanted to preserve their view of the park. They petitioned their sovereign who was persuaded to make do with iron railings which they paid for.

The 17th century house at number 14 was part of William Hooker's estate. It has some careful 18th century additions. Court musician John Lanier purchased the site, where numbers 16 to 24 stand, in 1505. A later occupant of 24 was 1984 novelist **George Orwell**'s wife who lived there during the 1939 to 1945 war.

Gloucester Circus with its attractive 18th century houses designed by Michael Searles joins the terrace from the right. The terrace was intended to provide an oval circus with two crescents looking onto a green but the north terrace was never built. Even so the circus is today very popular with film crews.

Numbers 26 to 36 Crooms Hill are late 17th century to mid 18th century houses and once housed French Huguenots fleeing from persecution as briefly described in novelist Daniel Defoe's novel *Roxanna*. Another resident was a certain Nicholas Wignall who is said to have left his wife "my second best teapot" in his will. Numbers 38 and 40 Crooms Hill are 19th century buildings. Houses have stood at numbers 42 to 48 since 1638. Erasmus Snelling built the houses which in the 1670s and 80s were occupied by Mark Cottle and a century later by the Olivier family. In 1813 Lancelot Loat bought the houses and demolished them to build houses for the working classes.

We then came to Grange House and the gazebo. These were built for Sir William Hooker, Sheriff of London, during the Great Plague of 1665 and the Great Fire of London which followed in 1666. In 1673 he became Lord Mayor of London. Being an owner of large estates in the Crooms Hill area he would probably have profited from the subsequent moves of the wealthy out of plague and fire ridden central London.

The cream coloured Grange was built first in 1665 and the now finely restored gazebo followed in 1672. The Grange was constructed on the site of Paternoster Croft which some say had been a gift from King Alfred's daughter to the Abbey of Ghent in 918. Sir William's wealth is shown by the house which had three coach houses and stabled eight horses. The gazebo was built almost on top of the road to ensure a fine view of the park.

The four storey May's Court was built a century later and was home to some of the first ever purpose-built flats. It has three main entrances, one of which has Ionic pillars. The others have rustications or masons' marks.

The oldest domestic house in Greenwich is believed to be at number 66, now Heathgate, but once known as Stella House and the Presbytery. The house had already been built by William Smith, a larger estate owner when in 1634 it was purchased by Dr Robert Mason. Mason's heirs would include Admiral Mason and the Mason who gave his name to the famous Mason-Dixon Line established in the USA.

The interior of Heathgate has been altered to form, with Hyde Cliff (built by one of the Mason family in 1696), part of the St Ursula's Convent school along with number 64. Known as Stobcross Lodge, number 64 was once the home of **James Thornhill** who created the fabulous Painted Hall in the Naval College. Another occupant was RS Jackson MP for Greenwich in the early 1900s.

At the summit we arrived at the base of the towering round spire which we could see as we climbed the hill. We had reached the church of **Our Lady Star of the Sea.** Much of the money to build the church was raised by weekly two-penny donations from the 500 Catholic pensioners residing at the Royal Hospital for Seaman, now the Royal Naval College. Completed in 1851, the church was designed by the architect, W.W.Wardell, a friend of Augustus and Edward Pugin who designed the interior. **Visits** are by appointment (tel 0208 858 0662), and there is **disabled access**.

Further along the road to the left where it forks are the 17th century Manor House, 19th Century Hillside and the early 18th century Park Hall. These were all on Sir William Hooker's estate. Park Hall was designed by John James, architect of St Alfege's church tower.

The east side of the park is bordered by Maze Hill road where **Maze Hill train station**, the closest station to the park, is located. Halfway up the hill is **Sir John Vanbrugh's** splendid symmetrical brick folly of castellated towers and turrets, **Vanbrugh Castle.** He built the 'castle' in 1719 while working at the Seamen's Hospital and lived there for seven years between 1719 and 1726.

Further down at 111 Maze Hill is the 18th century home of former black slave, **Olaudah Equiano** who aided the plan to send poor blacks off to Sierra Leone to set up a new life. At number 115 sits an equally old house with a blue plaque to commemorate former dweller, poet **Helena Pare Lydia Mott**.

Maritime Greenwich Town

Greenwich had long been an important port and had a thriving fish market at Fish Dock close to Greenwich Pier. In 1849 Grimsby Dock opened in the north but by 1900 Greenwich was finished as a fishing port. The opening of the foot tunnel to the north side of the river in 1902 also put paid to the Warner ferry service which had been crossing the Thames for over 200 years.

Nevertheless the development of industry in Greenwich and the growth of the Arsenal in Woolwich bolstered the area's importance. Maritime history is still very much celebrated in the Greenwich today.

In West Greenwich, the **Cutty Sark** stands beside King William Walk, the previous site of Church St noted for its beautiful 17th century houses. The houses deteriorated and were demolished in 1901 and the ship was brought to Greenwich in 1954. The boat Gypsy Moth VI stands on the old Brewhouse Lane.

Located by the river at the ferry terminus, the tall ship's masts of the Scottish built Cutty Sark rise above the ground giving great dignity to a sailing ship which in the 19th century was a mere Tea Clipper. Along Riverside Walk is the **Cutty Sark pub** on Ballast Quay, Built in 1804 it commands great views of the river.

Close by, the **Gypsy Moth IV** (tel 0208 858 3445) stands proudly as the boat in which the British sailor, **Sir Francis Chichester**, became the first to solo-circumnavigate the globe. He set sail on the 54ft ketch in August 1966 and returned in May 1967. Chichester was knighted here by the Queen using the same sword that Queen Elizabeth I is reputed to have used to knight the maritime adventurer, Sir Francis Drake.

The Cutty Sark (tel 0208 858 3445) is **open** for inspection Mon-Sat 10am-5pm, Sun noon-5pm with entry **costing** £3.50 per head.

It was built as a cargo ship, its name attributed to a legend related in a poem by Robbie Burns. On the bow of the ship is a witch holding a horse's tail. Legend has it that after a night of heavy drinking, Tam O'Shanter, while taking a short cut through a cemetery, stumbled across open graves. The corpses, a coven of witches, danced to the tunes of the devil.

> *There sat auld Nick, in shape of beast;*
> *A tousie tyke, black, grim, and large,*
> *To gie them music was his charge:*
> *He srew'd the pipes and gart them skirl,*
> *Till roof and rafters a' did dirl.-*
> *Coffins stood round, like open presses,*
> *That shaw'd the dead in their last dresses;*

The most beautiful of the hags was wearing a short chemise known as a cutty sark. Tam called out shouting her praises: "Well done the Cutty Sark!"

She heard his cry and chased him. Frightened Tam ran away, clambered onto his horse and headed for the river. It was said that the power of witches could not cross water. Just as he reached the banks the witch grabbed the horse by the tail. The tail came off and is depicted by the ship's bust clutching a horse's tail.

We entered the ship which once spliced its way across the oceans to China and as a wool carrier to Australia. Displays depict life as it would have been on board in 1869. The iron framed wooden ship with its three sailing masts also has a fine collection of 50 ship figureheads.

The Thames Barrier

We boarded the ferry at Greenwich Pier beside the Cutty Sark. With an old sea dog at the helm giving a running commentary and a good view of the river on the two storey chugger, it was one of the most pleasurable boat trips I'd ever had.

The captain informed us that the boat we were sailing on was a pleasure boat during the 1939-1945 war. When British troops had been driven back to Dunkirk by the German Armies it was called into action, with it being one of the fastest pleasure boats of its time. Tens of thousands of British soldiers required evacuation from **Dunkirk** requiring every boat possible to be summoned to cross the English Channel.

Our boat was one of them. It survived the shelling and brought back scores of soldiers which is why, according to the captain, the boat is allowed to fly the special ensign flag which can only be flown by boats and ships that sailed for Dunkirk.

"Behold the Thames river," he said, "It's the cleanest water in the world. All London drinks that water. The only water that you can drink and chew at the same time."

The water wasn't exactly crystal clear and we laughed as he informed us that we were off to see the eighth wonder of the world. Out in the centre of the river his point was given strength by the sight of the more common red teal. This was a rare sighting and a sign, of the improved water quality. Even herons and cormorants appeared diving for fish. The captain declared that there were more cormorants and herons in the Thames now than in Devon or Cornwall.

On our right lay the Trafalgar Tavern and, beyond it, a retirement home where no women are permitted to enter, even as staff. From here the Royal Naval College and the Royal Observatory in Greenwich Park were clearly visible.

Across the river on the north bank, a Jamaican tanker was offloading sugar to a Tate and Lyle refinery – a reminder of the maritime trade that had made London and Greenwich so wealthy.

Within five minutes the water level had risen by a foot. The captain drolefully announced that the water was about to reach the danger line, a vivid indication of the important role played by the Thames Barrier. The water levels had risen to flood levels several times recently and without the barrier parts of London would have been flooded. The south is dramatically being threatened by the sea. No better example was pointed out by the captain than the church on the north bank of the river in the borough of Tower Hamlets, now ten feet below our water line. Since the time of Elizabeth I, he claimed that the south had sunk six feet.

"The reason why I'm telling you this", he said, "is if you want to buy a luxury flat in London, don't buy one by the river. Buy one on the top of Shooters Hill or Plumstead Common."

We approached a huge Norwegian ship waiting to sail through the barrier on the otherwise peaceful river. To our left the captain pointed to the Isle of Dogs which he said had acquired its name because it was once the hunting ground of the kings.

Behind was **Canary Wharf Tower**, the second tallest building in Europe. The lights atop warn the planes about to land at London's City airport. The boat twisted with the meandering of the Thames and shortly the NatWest tower, the Post Office Tower and the top of St Paul's Cathedral came into view.

On our right, as we passed the **Millennium Dome**, the captain pointed to the hole in its roof. "It's the biggest hole in a roof in the world. That hole is there because they built the dome on top of Blackwell Tunnel and its air filters which takes all the toxic fuels out of the tunnel," he informed. "You would have thought with all that money being spent that they could have built it a few hundred feet away." He had a point.

He went on to tell us, "It's twice the size of Wembley Stadium. The twelve uprights are 300ft tall. The supports are so strong they could park a jumbo jet up there. Its high enough to fit in Nelson's Column and has enough space to store 18,000 double-decker buses and for Millwall soccer supporters 13 million barrels of lager would squeeze inside."

There'll be 100 toilets in the dome supplied by recycled rainwater generated on site. Very eco-friendly but if it's a very dry summer they'll need a few million plastic buckets!"

Beside the dome the captain pointed to the new **Jubilee Line** station which would soon be bringing tens of thousands of people to the Millennium Exhibition. Next door is **Trinity Wharf Lighthouse** one of the oldest lighthouses in Britain. Opposite the dome lies the River Lee connecting the Thames with the Grand Union Canal in the Midlands.

Just before the Barrier came into view the boat turned and we were presented with the photographer's dream – within one camera shot came London's tallest building, Canary Wharf, the Millennium Dome and St Paul's Cathedral.

We finally arrived at the Thames Barrier, beautifully architected with ten huge silver armadillos rising out of the choppy waters. With a touch of the Sydney Opera House in Darling Harbour, Australia, the structure spanned 520 metres across the width of the river. Ten separate movable gates are supported by concrete piers and the armadillos which operate the massive gates.

We went through barriers 8 and 9 on a small gate, weighing in at a mere 900 tonnes. Each of the four principal gates weighs 3,700 tonnes and stands as high as a five storey building, and as wide as the opening of Tower Bridge. In just over a decade the gates have closed over thirty times to protect the capital. Four small gates are suspended in the air while six larger gates are submerged beneath the water.

So serious is the threat of flooding that the banks and walls enclosing the Thames here have been raised by 12ft.

Disembarking at the Barrier and catching the next boat back is optional. We got off at the cafeteria on the south bank to view the **Visitors Centre** which houses an operating model of the Barrier and an informative video of its history. It also includes a children's play area for four to twelve year olds and a picnic area close to the Riverside Walk.

The Visitors Centre (tel 0208 395 4188) is open daily except between Xmas Eve and Boxing Day between 10am and 5pm on weekdays and 10.30am and 5.30pm at weekends. Admission is £3.40, £2 for children and over 65s with concessions for groups of 20 or more.

The **cruise** from Greenwich Pier (0208 305 0300) takes 25 minutes or 75 minutes if starting from Westminster (0207 930 3373). **Charlton train station** is 15 minutes walk away and the centre is on the nos. 177 and 180 **bus routes**.

A short walk down river, at Park Row, we arrived at the historic **Trafalgar Tavern** where a pub has stood for over 300 years. We stood inside with the ghosts of its previous reputed clients such as the highwayman **Dick Turpin** and **Dr Crippen** the murderer. **Dr Johnson** was also said to have dined here. Clearly so too did the celebrated British 19th century author, **Charles Dickens,** for he wrote a wonderful eulogy to the tavern in the novel *Our Mutual Friend* when describing a wedding feast.

We ascended the elegant staircase to the lavish Regency style banqueting suite known as the **Nelson Room** with room for 250 guests.

Here there were more historic shadows traipsing the entrance. Prime Minister **William Gladstone** and a century long list of high level government ministers would dine here at special regular events known as the **Whitebait Dinners**. Whitebait is a tiny fish which could be caught in the Thames and was popular with those who lived and worked on the Thames in the early 1800s with many of its eating establishments abel to serve whitebait within an hour of the fish being caught, Greenwich become famous for its whitebait meals.

The taste for the delicacy spread up river to the members of the parliament and by the time the Trafalgar Tavern opened in 1837, cabinet ministers were enjoying regular whitebait dinners in Greenwich. Around 1900 the practice died out but the tradition has been re-established and cabinet ministers have returned to dine annually, holding their whitebait dinner at the Trafalgar Tavern.

Upstairs is an elegant bar made out with all manner of ship's equipment and offering views of the Thames.

The Thames Barrier

The ground floor area recreates the Trafalgar Tavern in its heyday; a rough and ready inn for fishermen and ferrymen and popular with travellers. Today's clients come from far and wide to drink at what was the village's main drinking den in 1815.

The walls are cluttered with old paintings and sea going memorabilia. Sitting by the window we had an impressive view of the Thames which at high tide seemed ready to sweep in and engulf us. (**Open daily** from 11am with bar snacks and a la carte menu. Tel 0208 858 2437, fax 0208 858 2507.)

Another riverside pub of note is **The Yatch** (near the Trafalgar Tavern in Crane Street) beside which is the home of the **Globe Rowing Club**. Rowing has long been a popular sport in the area and **Greenwich Regatta** is said to be the oldest regatta in the world.

GREENWICH TOWN

Around Greenwich Town

Greenwich Market

With all its maritime and royal activity, Greenwich began to develop as a town and industrial growth came rapidly in the 19th century. The Thames loops at Blackwall. Here, right up till 1839, the fields would occasionally flood with the tides. A river wall was built but, with Greenwich ratepayers responsible for its upkeep (and sometimes defaulting) the wall was poorly maintained, resulting in floods and marshlands. The only road through was Marsh Lane which became Tunnel Avenue and later, Blackwall Lane.

Apart from a gibbet, the marsh had only two buildings in the 18th century. One was the **Watch House** used to house prisoners before they were sent to death at Execution Docks where they would be drowned under three tides. The other was the **New Magazine** which had been used since 1520 as a store for the Woolwich Yard gunpowder. Also known as the Powder Magazine, it was a source of many explosions. An Act of Parliament in 1780 removed the explosives to a hulk in the river.

An ironmaster named Crowley arrived at Ballast Quay in Greenwich in the early 18th century. He made ironware and had secured a monopoly in anchor making. He also made chains and manacles for the slave ships. His factories were located in northern England, but he wanted to be closer to the Thames' dockyards and shipbuilders. He built a massive warehouse on the edge of the marsh at Highbridge and began the industrialisation of the marsh.

The Enderby family who lived on Crooms Hill had accumulated a vast fortune from whaling. They constructed Enderby Wharf and built another for making rope situated next to Crowley's works. The Enderbys, whose whaling activities were mentioned in Melville's famous adventure, **Moby Dick**, were fascinated with nature and instructed their whaling captains to bring back botanical specimens from their voyages. Charles Enderby, who in 1838 had moved into Enderby

House, set up a natural History Museum and founded the **National Geographical Society**.

The Enderby's rope factory was destroyed by fire and the family moved to South America only to be greeted with further failure. The following owner of the site was Glass Elliot who used it to make cable. Here, the first Atlantic Cable was made. As Glass Elliot-Alcatel the business continues to supply cable to this day.

> *One spectacular business failure was that of an ex-army officer by the name of Alexander Theophilus Blakeley. Blakeley built the 'model cottages' known as Blakeley's Cottages for the workers in his gun factory. He exported guns to the Confederate pro-slave owner side in the American Civil War. The Galena Blakeley gun still stands on show in the USA as the gun that fired the opening salvo at Fort Sumter to begin the civil war. The Confederates lost and, paid in Confederate paper money. Blakeley, who is said to have been financed by Opium dealers, went bust.*

A chemical plant for making soap and extracting ammonia from coal gas was erected in the 1830s. The South Metropolitan Gas Works company built what was at the time the largest gas works in the world. Due to labour shortages London County Council began building houses such as Idenden Cottages in Blackwall Lane. Among the architects were George Smith, designer of the Morden College estate.

On Greenwich High Rd, **Greenwich Railway Station** was first erected in 1838. It was the last stop on the first suburban rail in the world. The grand imperial hype was for Greenwich High Rd to be called Empire Road whereby the railway line would cross Europe and go all the way to India. The line was planned in 1831 and reached Deptford five years later. The line now runs between Charing Cross and Gravesend in Kent.

The route from London Bridge Station required a viaduct to be built. The viaduct took 60 million bricks and more than 600 Irish and English bricklayers and labourers to build. Today it is still composed of 878 arches and supports the Southern Electric Line. By 1845 trains were running every 15 minutes to London.

Later the **Blackwall Tunnel** arrived resulting in the areas industrial decline. The whole area from Greenwich Pier to Church St had been a festering ghetto. Bought by compulsory purchase in the early 19th century, the houses were flattened. Only Turnpin Lane was left. The pier and the market were built and Nelson Road constructed.

GREENWICH TOWN

Saint Alfege Church

"St. Alfege was a bishop who was held in ransom. A Viking was sorry for the bishop who was having ox bones thrown at him and he killed the bishop with an axe. The bishop was buried in his home town, Canterbury."

Rebecca Hall (aged 9) on Greenwich Guide's children's ghost tour.

In the middle of Greenwich on Greenwich Church St towers the imposing neo-classical church of **Saint Alfege**. A church has existed on this site since the 10th century.

Saint Alfege was a bishop captured and held for ransom by invading Danes who had moored their long boats at Greenwich. Since Alfege was the Archbishop of Canterbury, the Viking warriors expected a large sum. Alfege opposed the payment and was taken to Greenwich. Some say he was clapped in irons in a damp cell frequented by frogs. They demanded a ransom of 3,000 marks from the king.

A plot was hatched and Alfege escaped only to fall into a bog, then recaptured. The Viking leaders held a council meeting to decide their ward's fate. Alfege was before them, sat down and manacled. As the meeting proceeded his capturers turned to drinking and eating.

Food and ox bones were thrown at Alfege. Alfege had converted some of the Viking warriors and, though one story has it that he was beaten to death by ox bones, another has it that one of his converts split his head open with an axe as an act of mercy. Later, King Canute, the English King who tried to order back the ocean, commanded that the bishop's remains be taken from London to Canterbury.

This imposing edifice was designed by Hawksmoor around 1712 after the second church to occupy the site had had been destroyed by a storm. In 1711 it was the first choice of 50 new churches commissioned for London. In 1730 the old tower was encased by John James.

17th century worshippers at St Alfege include diarists, **John Evelyn** and **Samuel Pepys**. Pepys wrote enthusiastically of the church which offered "a good sermon, a fine church and a great company of handsome women". While Henry VIII was baptised here Buried here are **Thomas Tallis**, the Tudor composer, General James Wolfe, John Julius Angerstein and Lavinia Fenton (Polly Peachum). The Thomas Thallis Society puts on **concerts** in the church (tel 0208 317 8687).

The church is **open for visitors** (tel 0208 853 0687) from April to October 12pm-3pm, and November to March, 12pm-2pm. **Disabled access**, but prior notice preferred.

St Alfeges Church, Greenwich

Accommodation

To the right stands the ***Mitre Hotel*** (tel 0208 293 0037 fax 355 6761, disability access), at 291 Greenwich High Rd. This pleasant Georgian building dates back to 1700 when the last building burnt down. The pub downstairs has been in existence since 1827 but the hotel rooms have been restored and only recently been made available for guests. The 15 bedrooms have *en suite* facilities and are non-smoking. Muriel, a smoker, went to stay the night to try out its facilities.

Her stay was enjoyable and she found the rooms with television, tea and coffee provided very pleasant. In the morning she enjoyed a full English breakfast in the attractive breakfast bar surrounded with old wooden panelling. The Mitre offer mainly bed and breakfast but lunch and dinner can be taken in their carvery.

Market, food, drink...

A well stood at one end of Stockwell St, formerly the town's market area. Today, the *Spread Eagle* restaurant (tel 0208 853 2333) stands in its place.

Greenwich Market (tel 0207 247 6590) opened centuries ago on Turnpin Lane. Walking down the narrow cobbled lane with its old houses we took care to walk on either side of the central gutter. In days of yore when sewage systems were considered luxuries, householders would toss their rubbish, dirty water, excrement and the like from their windows onto the street where the gutter would eventually channel the sewage down hill. With less than the width of a car between each side of the street, 'strolling down the lane' must have been a hazardous rather than romantic activity.

The lane was so named because it led to the turnpin where horses would be prevented from entering and people would queue to pay taxes. The lane was an extension of the main road into the town. It headed past the opposite turnpin at the *Cricketers Arms* (0208 858 3630) to Queen's House, then beyond to the old coach terminal on Stockwell St and on west. We popped into the Cricketers, a traditional pub which offers free admission to their **English folk music** night on Tuesday nights and **New Orleans jazz** on Sunday afternoons.

Turnpin Lane opens up to Greenwich Market which has been a market place for three centuries. The colonnades on the entrance opposite the lane bear the Royal Seal sanctioning the market given by King William IV.

The market side of the colonnades bears an inscription posted in 1831 as a warning to all market traders: "A false balance is abomination to the Lord, but a just weight is His delight."

The sign has not deterred the vendors for the covered market has over 160 stalls making it a bustling place attracting plenty of bargain hunters. Thursdays are ideal for **antique collectors** and weekends bring out **artists** and **designers**. There are also plenty of cafes and bars to sit down in, take a break or view the spectacle.

A shop worth popping into for photographers is *Fergus Noone Photography* (tel 0208 858 3309) with its displays of original photos of Greenwich.

...comedy and music

One recent addition to the Greenwich hall of fame is the *Up the Creek* comedy cabaret club at 302 Creek Rd. The club (tel 0208 858 4581) posts alternative comedy acts on Friday, Saturday and Sunday nights, with some of the country's leading alternative performers. The acts, hosted by the grand-daddy of alternative comedy, **Malcolm Hardy,** are followed on Fridays and Saturdays by a **disco** till 2am. Entry is £10 (Fri), £12 (Sat) and £6 (Sun) a head. Bar food is served.

Another recent young and trendy venue is the **Time Bar** (0208 305 9767) at 7A College Approach which doubles as a restaurant and art gallery. The furniture is minimalist and the stairs a chore to climb but once we had removed our oxygen equipment, boots and ice axes we were treated to a fine display of modern art and excellent coffee.

Also of note is **Rothbury Hall** (tel 0208 853 1336) on Azof St towards the Dome. A Grade 2 listed building, it was built in 1893 as a Congregational Mission Hall. The roofline is unique and it boasts a fine interior now used as an arts and theatre venue run by Greenwich local authority.

Walking down to number 9 Greenwich Church St I found Phillies Snack Bar (0208 853 5201) which serves Disotto's Italian Ice Cream. This inexpensive cafe has a friendly, relaxed atmosphere selling hot and cold snacks. Its speciality is its range of extra-light coffees in 20 different styles, and cappuccinos served flavoured with almond, orange, strawberry, caramel, cinnamon or practically anything you might wish. A good place to sit down and relax.

Further on at numbers 11-13, Greenwich Church St we came to the **Green Village** restaurant (tel 0208 858 2348) which, though specialising in kebabs also serves up a daily Sunday roast for £5 and **whitebait fish dinners.** With a sandwich house, chip shop, burger bar, and the **High Chaparal** restaurant all opposite Greenwich Market, visitors are offered a wide range of food which should keep the kids happy.

Further still is the **Spanish Galleon Tavern** just around the corner from Admiral

Hardy's pub. Turning right we came to William Walk which leads to the entrance of the Royal Naval College.

We sat in the **Funnel and Firkin** pub (tel 0208 305 2088) at 174 Greenwich High Rd is located next door to **Cafe Rouge** and beside the main post office. Being a standard Firkin pub they served cheap food, reasonable ales and had the occasional live music events. The lively **Prince of Orange** pub (0208 488 7123) at 188 Greenwich High Rd has **blues nights** on Thursdays, **funky soul nights** on Sundays and on Mondays, performances of the **Magnetic North Poets and Writers** (tel 0208 516 8646). Admission is free of charge.

Behind the pub at 189, Greenwich High St is the **Prince of Orange Theatre** (0208 858 9256) and Greenwich Railway Station.

Close by are **Greenwich Cinema** (tel 01426 919020) at 180 Greenwich High Rd, the popular **North Pole** restaurant (tel 0208 853 3020) at 131 and **Davy's Wine Vaults** (tel 0208 858 7204) at 161/165 also serving meals.

Pubs holding **quiz nights** include the **Admiral Hardy** (7, College Approach, Mondays); **Ashburnham Arms** (25 Ashburnham Grove, Tuesdays); **Cutty Sark Tavern** (Ballast Quay, Thursdays); **Hardys,** 92, Trafalgar Rd, Wednesdays), **Morden Arms** (1 Brand St, Wednesdays); **Plume of Feathers** (19 Vista Park, Wednesdays).

Drinkers outside the Cutty Sark pub on the River Thames

BLACKHEATH **Rebellions and Royals**

Just six miles from the city centre, Blackheath is one of the most beautiful areas of public open space in London. A vast green area, it is bordered by historic houses and Greenwich Royal Park. At its centre lies the elegant church and spire of All Saints Church. The name, Blackheath, is believed to have come from the words *black heath* when it lay on the Roman Old Dover Road leading up to the forest of Shooters Hill. Some say that the name derives from mass burials at the time of the Great Plague which decimated the capital's population in 1665, but there is little evidence of any mass graves beneath the common. Besides, the name was established long before the 17th century.

The 1381 Poll Tax Revolt

In 1381, Wat Tyler, a Dartford blacksmith, and Jack Straw from Essex led the Great Peasants' Rebellion against the Poll Tax. Such a tax, levying similar amounts of money from all citizens, was re-introduced in Britain by Prime Minister Margaret Thatcher in 1989 causing a similar revolt. Feelings against Thatcher's tax led to 14 million people refusing to pay. Many of those refusing to pay the tax were thrown into prison but when Thatcher resigned the tax was revoked.

In 1381 the people of England were outraged at having to pay an extra tax levied at three groats per person over the age of 15. The levy ignited a massive armed revolt and Wat Tyler brought an army of 100,000 peasants and artisans onto the heath to confront the troops of Richard II. One group marched down and took control of the Tower of London. Another burned the Temple Library while a third destroyed the Monastery of St John at Clerkenwell. The revolt was eventually crushed. Tyler is said to have been killed by the sword of the Lord Mayor of London. Jack Straw and many other rebels were beheaded.

Centuries ago the heath was the last stop before entering London from the south. Many monarchs and their entourages would encamp on the open pastures, the scene of many great battles. In the early 1300s, the heath was

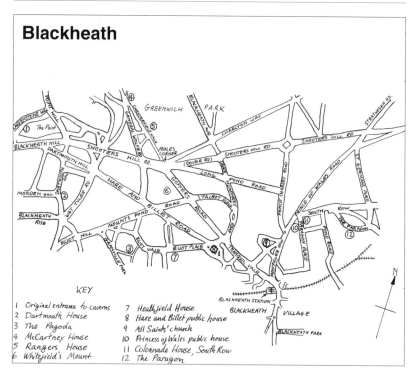

Blackheath

KEY

1 Original entrance to caverns	7 Heathfield House
2 Dartmouth House	8 Hare and Billet public house
3 The Pagoda	9 All Saints' church
4 McCartney House	10 Princess of Wales public house
5 Rangers House	11 Colonnade House, South Row
6 Whitfield's Mount	12 The Paragon

chosen as the venue where Isabella the Fair would arrive with her retinue to meet her bridegroom, **Edward II**. **Richard II** was met here by the heads of the city of London when returning home from war with his new wife, the daughter of the French king.

Merrier scenes followed at the beginning of the 1400s. **Henry V** and his army were received by the Lord Mayor of London and taken in triumph into the capital. The English king had just won an overwhelming victory over the French armies at the **Battle of Agincourt**. It tickled me to discover that among his warrior knights who had fought in France was none other than John Frampton. Much later, his heir, Tregonwell Frampton, would be Keeper to the Running Horses of William III, Queen Anne, George I and George II.

In the 1420s, Humphrey, Duke of Gloucester and youngest brother of the dead Henry V, had taken over the Manor of Greenwich. In Greenwich he built himself a palace and married. The duke had fought well at Agincourt where, having been wounded, he was saved by Henry VI. Henry VII acceded to the throne at such an early age that for a time, Humphrey (as uncle to the king) was Protector of England and the key voice in the land. He married his mistress Eleanor Cobham who, like her husband, had an interest in the occult.

'Mark'd for the Gallows' – The Men of Kent

Eleanor, Duchess of Gloucester, was convicted of sorcery and imprisoned after being forced to do a series of humiliating public acts as penance.

In 1447 her husband, Humphrey, was also arrested and later died. Five of his supporters were hung drawn and quartered. His death led to a great deal of discontent and the men and women of Kent rose up, led by the scarlet clothed Jack Cade.

Many nobles supported Jack Cade when he led his 'Men of Kent' against the king and encamped on Blackheath in 1450. They laid before the Royal Council the Blackheath Petition, demanding that they, "punish evil ministers and procure a redress of grievance."

The rebels killed the King's Leader who, according to Shakespeare, called them "rebellious hinds, the filth and scum of Kent, mark'd for the gallows". They then stormed London, killing the Lord Treasurer and destroying many title deeds and evidence of property with the aim of achieving universal equality.

The revolt was defeated and with a general pardon many rebels deserted. Cade was captured, hung drawn and quartered, and portions of his body displayed on the heath.

Rebellion ensued in 1452, this time from Richard, Duke of York. The king sent an army of 15,000 to the heath to conclude a peace with York's army. Later that year King Henry would again return to the heath with his troops to block the advancing army of his rebellious cousin, Edward.

The final rebellion of this turbulent century occurred in 1497 when the **Cornish Peasants' Revolt** against taxes took place, bringing thousands of armed Cornishmen onto the heath. Warbeck, claimant to Henry VII's throne and said to be a spitting image of Edward IV, allied with the King of Scotland and invaded England. Henry levied a tax to raise £120,000 from the English peoples. The people of Cornwall violently objected to paying the tax for a distant war. **Lord Audley**, related to the House of York (Henry VII was from the line of the opposing House of Lancaster), installed himself at the head of the Cornish armed uprising.

The Cornish Peasants' Revolt

The Cornish army, inspired by Thomas Flammock and Michael Joseph, marched to London hoping to gain support, particularly from Kent. They found few willing allies and reached Blackheath rather dispirited but prepared to do battle. From his palace at Greenwich, Henry had raised an army ready to move north to aid Lord Darby, leading the fight against the Scottish and Warbeck. The king moved his forces down to Deptford, with 25,000 troops massing. On June 17 they engaged battle with the Cornishmen at Deptford Bridge. Half the royal troops faced the rebels at the bridge while others arrived at the rear. By noon the Cornish, armed only with pikes, had been defeated and returned to Blackheath.

Between 600 and 2,000 Cornishmen were slaughtered and said to have been buried under Whitfield's Mount. The rebels sued for peace and received an official pardon, agreeing to pay the tax and an additional tax to pay for the army raised against them. Lord Audley was captured, escaped and later recaptured. Taken to the Tower of London he was tried for treason, and executed wearing a paper suit of armour and a paper Yorkist crown. The defeat was seen as the last attempt by the House of York to seize the throne.

The rebellion is celebrated by a Cornish slate plaque on the James II wall beside Greenwich Park gates, in memory of Michael Joseph, a very well educated smithy, Thomas Flammock and Lord Audley.

Greyfriars Monastery was the first in England to be closed during **Henry VIII**'s 'Dissolution of the Monasteries'. In a struggle against the power of the Papacy, Henry was determined to divorce his queen, **Katharine of Aragon**. The Pope objected as did the Abbot of Greyfriars. The heath would play another part in this period of English history in 1540 when it was the reputed location of Henry VIII's first planned encounter with **Anne of Cleves**. The king is said to have walked hand in hand with her back to his palace. However, Henry boycotted the meeting.

The historian Burke has her contemporaries describing the German Princess, Anne of Cleves as, "the big fat woman who did not look like a queen", and "tall, with coarse features, had ugly hands and feet, a large mouth, and bad teeth....a vulgar appearance and ungraceful manners."

Part of a political marriage conjured up by Archbishop Cranmer, the couple looked a sorry sight at their wedding. Henry, quotes Burke, "seems more like a widow at the grave of his better-half than a bridegroom". It was added, "Someone will suffer in the skin and hide for giving him this greasy-faced Jack for a wife."

First, Anne of Cleves paid. She was 'unmarried', ordered to return all her wedding presents and newly described as the king's 'sister'. The others including Cranmer would pay later with their heads. However when Henry's next wife, Catherine Howard, was executed, Anne was able to exclaim, "Good Heaven, what an escape I had!"

When relative peace finally returned to the heath leisure became its biggest renown. In 1585 **Queen Elizabeth I** used Blackheath to review her trained bands. The Stuart, **King James I**, who lived at Greenwich Palace, is reputed to have brought the sport of golf to England, playing his first round at Blackheath. Originally a Scottish and French sport it had been played by James who was also King James VI of Scotland.

However his handicap was set back when civil war ensued in Britain, once again bringing turmoil to the heath. No real battles in the English Civil War of 1642 to 1649 were fought on the heath but in 1648, Cromwellian General Fairfax confronted an advance guard of Royalist troops there, forcing their retreat all the way to Maidstone where they were routed.

Peace returned and while many troops would still camp and drill on the heath, golf flourished. In 1754 **Royal Blackheath Golf Club** became the first to be established in the world. The 19th century building on Talbot Place near Whitefield's Mount was, for a short time after 1910, a clubhouse for the players.

Right up until 1921 the men would play in bright scarlet coats warning others on the heath. Their caddies were able bodied pensioners from Greenwich Hospital and paid six pence a day, a pint of porter and a pie. Forward caddies even carried red flags. Golfers were either members of the Summer or Winter (Knuckle) Clubs which eventually merged. By the 1880s a 9-hole course cut across the common. The clubs had rules for negotiating various hazards, for example a ball being stuck in a gas lamp, in a moving vehicle or garden.

After the 1914-18 war so many more people were using the heath that London County Council were forced to limit the hours of play. The club merged with Eltham Golf Club and moved away from the heath to Eltham Lodge.

Another popular English sport which came early to the heath was **cricket**. By the 1860s an estimated 60 cricket matches could be taking place simultaneously. Pitches would increasingly overlap causing confusion for the players and the general public. The Hare and Billet team of 'Gentlemen and employed players' was considered the most prestigious. The team had a wicket near the end

The heath at Blackheath.

of Eliot Place and opposite the Hare and Billet pub and posted 'minders' to protect their patch. Later their name changed to West Kent Wanderers. A **Hare and Billet** pub remains.

One of the Wanderers' celebrated players was Nicholas Wanostroct, a Camberwell teacher who moved to South Row on the heath. He also played county cricket for Kent and Surrey. Publishing a book on the subject, he was considered to be one of the sport's founding fathers. "Felix on the Bat" had sketches of how to play various strokes and comments on how 'gentlemen' should conduct themselves.

Between 1780 and 1798, archery became fashionable on the heath. The Duke of Buccleuch who lived on the heath set up a men's archery club which was challenged and defeated by the heath's ladies' British Amazons club in 1791.

Illegal bareknuckle fighting bouts used to take place on the heath surrounded by scores of onlookers. Bouts would be between 'fighters' or between 'gentlemen' who would engage in the fisticuffs for a wager or sponsor the fighters. Known as mills, these bouts which engaged famous warriors like **Tom Cribb**, were held in secret with their location being passed around south London by word of mouth. Sometimes the police would intervene until the Marquess of Queensbury established rules and the sport was legalised.

Leg-men (bookies' touts) would shout out the odds round by round to the blacklegs (gamblers) who would shout out their nuller (fighter) and place their roll of soft (wads of notes).They could easily end up feather to fly (broke) if the fight was a cross (fixed) or they were fleeced by dummy hunters (pickpockets). Fighting was brutal and Tom Cribb fought his first fight over 76 rounds (a round was a knock down). Cribb also fought a championship fight in one of the gravel pits which left his opponent dead.

Shinty (a hockey-like game) was a pretty brutal sport introduced to the heath by Scottish soldiers staying at Woolwich Barracks. The wild sport was often played between rival clans. With almost no rules to the game, it brought many injuries and one game would see more substitutes than players starting the game. A popular spectator sport accompanied by drunken revelry, it was played on the heath from 1750 but eventually banned in 1810 and moved to Charlton Marsh.

Other sports such as horse riding, ice skating on the ponds and later, cycling, came to the heath. The **Horse Protection League** of Blackheath imposed a ban on horses on the heath. They were also said to be responsible for the (still operational) bye-laws governing donkeys' working hours on the heath (20 walks up and down, 30 minutes rest and three hours in total).

Blackheath Rugby Club (tel 0891 715 400) lays claim to being the oldest rugby club in the world. Its origins lay in the Blackheath Proprietory School Old Boys Club which used to play on the heath. Its ground and clubhouse at Rectory Field were the venue for international matches before Twickenham became the national team's home in 1907. Today, the club remains one of England's foremost. Nowadays there is also a women's team, the **Blackheath Women's Rugby Club** (0208 858 1578), at the same address.

Until its closure the **Green Man** pub, which listed Tom Cribb among its clientele, attracted those keen on **bowling** which included many famous names. **Jonathan Swift** cited it in *Gulliver's Travels* as the place where the Lilliputian cattle were put to graze.

Common Land

Blackheath is sometimes wrongly called Blackheath Common. Strictly speaking 'common land' was owned with common rights for the people whereby, apart from pigs who threatened the soil with their rooting, animals could be grazed. Firewood could be gathered on the 'Bleak Heath' and trees cut for fuel. No digging for stones or minerals was permitted nor any fencing of land or house building.

Rather than common land, Blackheath is 'manorial waste'. For centuries it was the manorial waste of Lewisham, Kidbroke and Charlton, and leased by the lords for various uses. It became a public open space when the Lords of the Manors temporarily surrendered their manorial rights.

Fairs were held originally on a weekly, monthly or annual basis as granted by charter. Mostly trade fairs, they included horse, cattle, produce sales and the hiring of servants. Later the fairs broadened out with the increasing arrival of food and drinks stalls, gambling games, theatre and later still swings and roundabouts.

Gypsies would come twice a year before and after the Greenwich Fair. On the heath they would watch cock fights, bull and bear baiting and later boxing. But the heath wasn't only used for leisure pursuits. Military reviews would take place. For centuries the area facing Lloyds Place was used as a drying ground for drying laundry by the community of washerwomen who lived in a small built up area of the village. The Drying Ground remained as a designated area up until 1901. From 1670 until 1832 the heath also sported several windmills and Blackheath Vale had a brewery associated with it.

Beneath the pastures stretching into Greenwich Park lie layers of pebble beds, coarse sand, gravel and then chalk. Consequently, the soil was poor support for woodlands, instead giving rise to scrubs and gorse until it was finally turned into pastures. Today the heath supports 112 varieties of plants. Once there were many hollows and dips in the heath partly created due to excavations for sand and gravel. Rain also percolated through the soil till it reached the clay creating subsidence. Underground caverns would suddenly collapse occasionally taking people in their carts with them. The area was levelled when the hollows and dips were mainly filled in with rubble cleared from London bomb sites after the 1939-45 war.

Some of the ponds remain including the one close to Whitefields Mount and Folly Pond outside the park gates, formed when high class gravel (popular for paths) was dug. **Hares Billet** pond was partly supplied by a natural spring. **Blackheath Cavern** is a very large hole close to the surface but completely underground at Pount Hill. The cavern was created by chalk excavations in the 1600s which entered the ground in Maidstone Hill. A series of caverns around 12ft high with layers of flint and chalk have been discovered running parallel to Blackheath Hill, the last containing a well.

Dug in blocks then wetted, allowing it to slip along the underground roadway, the chalk was hauled out through a shaft. Next it was burnt creating calcium oxide (popularly known as lime) which was used to fertilise soil, for building mortar, whitewashing, bleach and disinfectant. Only when Sir John Morden took control of the land and sealed the caves in 1700 did excavations stop. The caves were re-opened 80 years later as recreation for local society such as the Hellfire Club who would hold events inside.

A small carving with a devil's head added to the attraction, and posters suggesting that the caves were once the scene of terrible deeds by Saxon warriors were displayed. The entrance fee was 6p per head. In 1854 a disaster occurred at a masked ball held in the caves. Somebody turned off the lights and caused a panic in which a reveller was killed, and several people were injured. The entrance was sealed and never again open to the public.

With Manorial rights, the Legge family, Earls of Dartmouth ordered open cast quarrying for chalk on the south side of Blackheath Hill. Other pits were created in various ways.

The only raised part of the heath is **Whitefields Mount** which is now a nature conservation area. It is believed to have been a pre-historic burial ground but others have suggested it is part of a Saxon burial ground. Blackheath was once renown for it s variety of animal life. Today the only known survivor of distinction is the Blackheath stag beetle which has a lighter hue than normal. A preacher in the illegal Dissenters' Movement, Methodist George Whitefield and then **John Wesley,** are said to have addressed crowds of 20,000 people from the mount which previously bore the name of Wat Tyler's Mount Jack Cades Mount, Cornish Mount and Mortar Mount (in the 17th century it was used to test mortars) reflecting the heath's rich history.

William Gladstone, the nineteenth century politician and prime minister and sometime Member of Parliament for Greenwich, spoke on the heath and on occasion was known to speak for over two hours on issues such as 'the Bulgarian Question'. Today, it is the preachers who hold sway and every Easter Friday you can still listen to a service here. Whitefield and Gladstone used their powerful voices but today the ecclesiastics are aided by a public address system.

Gladstone served as a government minister for 35 years. Known as the 'Grand Old Man' of British politics he supervised the expansion of the British empire. He once accused a bishop of speaking, *"a combination of adroit claptrap and oracular rhodomontade"*. The diplomat is best known for his remark, *"Standing up to one's enemies is commendable, but give me the man who can stand up to his friends."*

Royalty, poll tax rebels, armies, brigands, Chartist revolutionaries, striking workers, suffragettes have all been associated with the heath, but today recreation has finally won out. The heath is popular at weekends for **kite flying** and we saw kites of all shapes and sizes floating in the breeze. But we couldn't spend too long gazing at the skies, as around us scurried **land yachts** – wind-propelled go-karts. Model planes are forbidden to fly but **model boats** sail in the Prince of Wales pond. There are plenty of regular **soccer** and **cricket** matches to watch.

The Waste - Ranger's House

The regal, red brick, Ranger's House besides Chesterfield Walk on the west side of the heath is one of five houses built illegally in Greenwich Park on land seized by Andrew Snape. Later Snape, a sergeant at arms in the palace, secured a 60-year lease on the land from the Crown.

Ranger's House was built for Captain (later Vice-Admiral) **Francis Hosier** between 1700 and 1720. However, Admiral Hosier never had the chance to settle in his new home. In 1726 he set sail to fight the Spanish fleet in the Caribbean. Close to Porto Bello his ships' crews succumbed to yellow fever and Hosier died with most of his crew in 1727. He was buried in St Nicholas Church in Deptford.

A later victory over the Spaniards at the same spot was commemorated with a ballad immortalising Hosier, *"Admiral Hosier's Ghost."* The song spoke of the victorious Admiral Vernon's fleet being haunted by Hosier's men who emerged from the ocean begging Vernon's crews to avenge them, thereby releasing the dead men from eternal mourning.

Hosier was the son of a ship's chandler from Deptford. As a young lieutenant, his fate was embroiled with a ship called HMS Neptune. The young man would later serve on another Neptune which explains Neptune's appearance over the front door to the house. The original house consisted only of the central red brick portions. They contrast with the later additions, the extra brown brick bays. Hosier's death brought about wranglings between the heirs and an inventory still exists of all the possessions of the house at the time.

By 1741 the house had become the property of the Rt Hon. John Stanhope, who died in 1748, leaving the property to be occupied by his elder brother **Philip, 4th Earl of Chesterfield**. Architect Isaac Ware had built the Earl's property in Mayfair and was brought in to enlarge Ranger's House. Ware designed the long gallery on the south side.

Chesterfield was initially reluctant to use the house but, growing increasingly deaf, the Earl spent more and more of his time at the house. He took to writing and gardening and leased more land from the Crown to increase the size of his gardens. Chesterfield was known for the letters he scribed to his heir and his illegitimate son with advice on life. In one such letter Chesterfield said that spelling "is so absolutely necessary for a man of letters, or a gentleman, that one false spelling may fix a ridicule upon him for the rest of his life."

Though reputed to have helped **Dr Johnson** with his dictionary, it seems Dr Johnson's gratitude was in doubt. Johnson wrote of Chesterfield, "....he has the manners of a dancing master and the morals of a whore". Despite Johnson's accusations, Chesterfield became Member of Parliament for two Cornish boroughs, and later Ambassador to The Hague, Lord Lieutenant of Ireland and Secretary of State.

The addition of the north bay, built to balance Chesterfield's south bay, was ordered by **Richard Hulse** who purchased the house after the Earl's death in 1773. As deputy director of the **Hudson Bay Company**, Hulse held a powerful position and played an important role in building the British Empire in North America.

The next occupant of the now panelled house, still then known as **Chesterfield House**, was Augusta, Duchess of Brunswick and sister to George III. She moved in during 1807 after her husband and later died when her daughter Princess Caroline lived in **Montague House** next door. In 1815, while Caroline was travelling abroad, Montague House was demolished. Chesterfield House was taken over by the crown and used as a grace and favour residence for the holder of the post of Ranger of the Park. The post was a sinecure and

BLACKHEATH

Montague House

gift of the monarch who invited them to use Ranger's House as their residence.

Montague House was bought by **Lord Montague** in 1702. In 1799 it became the residence of **Princess Caroline**, wife to the Prince Regent who would become **King George IV**. Another troubled Princess of Wales and one of the great characters of the borough, her previous home had been the Old Rectory in Fairfield Road, Charlton.

Caroline was disapproved of in royal circles even before she arrived in England. The Earl of Malmesbury who went to Brunswick in order to bring the Prince of Wales' fiancee to London described Caroline as, "*stockily built, dressed dowdily, spoke too much and coarsely, lacked moral reticence and good sense and washed so seldom that she was malodorous.*"

George already had a mistress, Mrs Fitzherbert to whom he was secretly married. Offered the clearing of his debts, a doubling of his income and a fully government-subsidised wedding ceremony, the Prince of Wales reluctantly agreed to marry his cousin Caroline.

When Caroline landed in England at Greenwich, the Prince of Wales declined to go and greet her, sending his Lady in Waiting, a former mistress, instead. The Lady in Waiting was late and Caroline had to kick her heels waiting in the Seamen's Hospital. On first seeing her the Prince declared he was unwell and asked for a glass of brandy. George lived with Caroline for only a short time, although sufficient to secure an heir to the throne and **Princess Charlotte** was duly born.

BLACKHEATH

The spurned Caroline resided in Montague House where her life was said to be defiantly, "all glitter and glare and trick, tinsel and trumpery." One report reads, "...the Princess is grown very coarse and that she dresses very ill, showing too much of her naked person..." However, Prime Minister **William Pitt** was so impressed by the Princess that he described her as "an enchanting princess who dwells in an enchanted palace".

In 1802, when Caroline is thought to have secretly given birth to an illegitimate son, the Princess refurbished the house. Her *joie de vie* is reputed to have led to indiscrete liaisons with various men. Among these were Sir Thomas Lawrence, painter of her portrait which is now owned by the Queen. Lawrence was thought to be her lover and the father of William Austin. The young politician George Canning and her Italian major domo were also said to be among her conquests. After he had become Prime Minister in 1827, Canning would write his *Ode to Gossip* including these lines;

> *All twattling grandmamma of lies!*
> *Thou darling of the Quidnunc throngs!*
> *With twice ten thousand ears and eyes*
> *And ten times twice ten thousand tongues.*
>
> *O! How I venerate thy power;*
> *For lo! Thou knowest everything –*
> *The secrets of the loneliest bower –*
> *The Councils of the mightiest king.*
>
> *Thou knowest if Robin kiss'd last night*
> *Old Farmer Hodge's pretty daughter;*
> *Thou never fail'st to "take a sight"*
> *When George goes to Virginia Water.*

The scandals led to the Delicate Investigation of 1806 which, at least officially, cleared her name of some of the more trumped-up allegations. Despite her trial, Caroline remained very popular in the locality. She continued to hold parties for young children at the house. One of the children, William Austin, said to be of a poor Deptford family, was adopted by the Princess sparking rumours that William was the illegitimate son.

Caroline's Party

*In 1808 a newspaper reported on a party that was given by
Caroline in Blackheath in honour of her mother, the Duchess
of Brunswick. Among those present were Sir Thomas and
Lady Wilson from Charlton House and Mr Angerstein from
Woodlands. The party was reported as "...the most splendid
and elegant entertainment that has been witnessed during
the present season. All the nobility and gentry remaining in
town together with those of the surrounding country, were
invited.*

*Forty covers were laid in the dining room and at 6.30,
seven persons of distinction sat down to a most sumptuous
dinner, served up in an elegant service of plate; the sideboard
was richly laid out with a number of large gold waiters and
salvers – the centre of the table was much admired for the
richness of the golden vases it contained filled with the choicest of aromatic flowers.*

*As soon as the company entered the dining room the band
belonging to the Royal Artillery struck up 'God Save the King'
and was followed by 'Rule Britannia' and several other delightful airs during dinner. At 10, the dancing began in the green-
house, which was prepared for the purpose – the walls and
ceilings were lined with the choicest shrubberies and flowers,
and enriched with wreaths and variagated lamps, a beautiful
chandelier hung in the centre, and over the door in the garden
were three large letters, A.D.B., in variagated lamps. The
lawn had a beautiful effect, the trees and shrubberies being
hung with lamps.*

*At 1.30am the company sat down to supper, and did not
break up until near four, when the company began to with-
draw. Her Royal Highness the Duchess of Brunswick seemed
highly pleased, and did not retire till near 12 o'clock, though
in general she goes to bed at 9.30. The Princess of Wales,
who was elegantly attired, seemed highly gratified, and her
endeavours to liven the scene were unremitting. The Ladies
vied with each other in splendour of dress. Miss Percival wore
a robe of pink satin, covered with a tunic of the most superb
Brussels net. Mrs B Paget wore a most elegant white satin
dress, richly embroidered with gold spangles."*

BLACKHEATH

BLACKHEATH

King George and Princess Caroline

In 1815 the Prince Regent put an end to Caroline's hedonistic getherings. Montague House was in a poor state of disrepair and was ordered to be demolished whilst she was abroad. Caroline returned to England, only to be rejected once again by her husband. A Bill of Pains and Penalties was drafted to strip Caroline of her rank due to her alleged misconduct abroad. A public enquiry brought great national support for her, including women wearing white bows in their hair to display their belief in the Princess's innocence. Caroline was subsequently acquitted bringing widespread celebration.

George became king and undeterred, he had Queen Caroline barred from his Coronation. Caroline died within weeks. The cause of death was given as, "stoppage of the bowels".

The first Ranger at Ranger's House was **Princess Sophia Mathilda**. The last of many titled occupants were Prince Arthur of Connaught, studying at Woolwich, followed by **Field Marshal Viscount Garnet Wolseley** who vacated the house in 1896. Sir Garnet Wolseley's name is celebrated in the army. He was a stickler for neatness and good order and there is a saying in the army, 'All Sir Garnet,' meaning all in order.

The house lay in disrepair till careful restoration by London County Council who also made it available for use as changing rooms for sports clubs. Today Ranger's House is an English Heritage property and on the ground floor houses the Suffolk collection of 16th and 17th century family portraits by famous artists. **Thomas Howard, 1st Earl of Suffolk,** commanded the fleet which sailed against the **Spanish Armada** in 1588. He had strong connections with maritime Greenwich. When the 19th Countess of Suffolk left for her native America she left the collection of family portraits to her daughter-in-law Mary Howard. Ms Howard decided that, in line with the 1st Earl's links with Greenwich, that the collection should be housed in Greenwich.

The paintings on view are those which were not sold off at various auctions, their positioning varying with time. Jacobean and early 16th century portraits were collected by the 15th Earl. Some, with exquisite costume detail, are attributed to William Larkin. Sir Godfrey Knellor, Sir Peter Lily and Sir Anthony Van Dyke's studio are said to have produced the portraits of the Stuart court. The famous painter, **Thomas Gainsborough,** is said to have painted the portrait of the 4th Earl, while Sargent painted that of the 19th Countess.

From the Large Stone Hall we passed through the Crimson Camblet Parlour before entering Lord Chesterfield's Gallery. The doorway into the gallery was constructed from what was once a window in the original Hosier house. The gallery extends the whole length of the original house. Heavily worked in plaster, the ceiling has Chesterfield's garter star at the centre. The floor boards, wide in the centre of the room then thinning towards the edges, create an impression of perspective. At the east end is an 1814 cabinet in English Oak by George Bullock.

Interestingly on the north wall the twins, Anne Cecil, Countess of Stamford, and Diane Cecil, Countess of Oxford, have identical dresses slashed to display their underskirts.

Leaving the Gallery we went into the Green Silk Damask Room or parlour with its portraits of Kings Charles I, Charles II and James II, Catharine of Braganza and Mary of Modena. Moving on to the large Dining Room we found various portraits, including that of Henry Howard who was simultaneously Earl of Berkshire and Earl of Suffolk. Off the Dining Room was situated the small Dressing Room.

Another house built on the land squatted by Snape is **Macartney House**. We visited the house which is famous as the former home of **General James Wolfe**, Commander of the British imperial campaign to conquer Canada. The Wolfes moved to Greenwich when James was 11 years old. They first lived in Straightsmouth while the young James attended Weston's Academy. In 1741, at the age of 14 James received his commission. His father bought the house in 1751 for £3,000 and for the next eight years it was James' home.

After the Wolfes left McCartney House Lord Lyttleton took up residence, extending the house to the rear. In 1810 Soane added a bay window overlooking Greenwich Park. The flats on the left overlooking the park were added in 1925 when the house was converted into apartments.

(Opening times; 1 April to 30 Sep, 10am-6pm, 1 Oct to 21 Oct, 10am-5pm, 22 Oct to 31 March, Wed-Sun 10am-4pm, closed 24-26 Dec. Entry Adults £2.50, children £1.30, concessions £1.90. Tel. 0208 853 0035 for further details)

Morden College and the Wricklemarsh Estate.

We crossed to the eastern end of the heath. Before us was a red sign announcing the Cator Estate and its private roads. John Cator, who bought property in the area in 1783, was the last man to expropriate part of the heath. We were at Morden College named after the wealthy **Sir John Morden**. John Morden was a wealthy merchant who traded in silks and spices around the Middle East. He had obtained his knighthood by lending money to King Charles II and purchased the Manor of Wricklemarsh in the 1660's so that he could remain in the countryside while still being close to the city.

General James Wolfe

BLACKHEATH

At the age of 14 years James Wolfe received a commission becoming an officer of the 1st Marine Regiment. By the time the soldier was 32 he had been appointed commander of the Canada campaign and a major general. In 1756 King Frederick II of Prussia invaded Saxony sparking a war between England and Prussia on one side and France, Austria and Spain on the other. Fighting spread to the colonies and the French under Montcalm won many victories over the English in Canada.

Wolfe had been posted to fight in the Canada campaign. Returning for a break in 1758, he was called to see the Prime Minister and was given command of the campaign. The Prime Minister was so shocked by Wolfe's boastful aggression that he declared, "Good God, that I should have entrusted the fate of my country to this man."

In February, 1759 James Wolfe left Blackheath for Quebec to lead the war against the French. His success was such that in the decisive battle on the Heights of Abraham the British were victorious seizing Quebec. Montcalm died in the fighting and so did Wolfe who was hit three times by musket balls. As Wolfe lay dying he is said to have called to his officers, "Support me – let not my brave soldiers see me drop. The day is ours. Keep it." On November, 1759 Wolfe's body was brought back to Blackheath to lie in state. In order to avoid a commotion, his body was then taken at midnight to be buried at St Alfege's Church.

Prior to Morden the Manor of Wricklemarsh had passed through several hands and had been mentioned in the Domesday Book written in 1086, an account of the estates of England for the Norman Conquerors. In the book, Wricklemarsh, mainly marshland and pastures was said to be a small estate with a small population and a wood for 15 pigs. In 1503 the estate was bought by Sir William Ganoway for the purpose of a building a house. He died without heirs and the estate was bought by the Blounts.

At the time of Cromwell, **Sir Thomas Blount** was lord of the manor and the tiny Blackheath village was known as Blunt's Hole. A Roundhead parliamentarian and a rabid puritan, he is said to have nevertheless planted a vineyard on the estate to create Wricklemarsh wine. An inventive chap, he created carriage suspension and an early milometer, he called a 'waywizer'. Blount also advocated rabbit farms arguing that these perennial breeders would feed the population more cheaply. His custom built rabbit warren came to nought.

In 1660, the Restoration of the monarchy saw his political retirement to Wricklemarsh. Hundreds of Puritans flocked to hear the local vicars protestant sermons. In 1667, the Anglicans considereing such speeches to be dangerously close to inflammatory, complained to Charles II who imprisoned Blount on suspicion of protecting the vicar. Pardoned, he returned to the estate. Morden bought the estate from him for £5,800, demolished Blount's house and built Morden House.

Legend has it that Morden packed three ships full of goods in Turkey sending them on to London. He travelled separately across Europe with the intention of doing the Grand Tour of Europe's great cities. Morden's trading ships laden with merchandise were lost. Their disappearance left the trader in financial ruin. In poverty he had to sell everything up to his creditors. But, as luck would have it, Morden, working as a waiter, overheard three customers talking of three ships that had mysteriously turned up after a long voyage. From the Mediterranean, the ships had turned left instead of right after passing the Straits of Gibraltar. In thanksgiving for the return of his riches, Morden arranged for an almshouse to be founded after his death, looking after 'decayed Turkey merchants' (meaning importers from Turkey).

Morden College was founded and built in the Wren style with four storeys of bay windows topped by a weathervane. The ominous red hand of William of Orange sits in the heraldic symbol. The builder is thought to have been Edward Strong, Wren's stonemason. To the left of the college entrance, we took the footpath beginning at St German's Place and found an excellent place to view the college. Jack Spratt, Bishop of Rochester, consecrated the college chapel. His name was given to the poem that began: '*Jack Spratt could eat know fat, his wife could eat no lean...*'

However, building work began with a hiccup. On Morden's death it was discovered that the income from his estates was hardly sufficient to keep his widow. Part of the Wricklemarsh Manor estate had to be sold off to maintain the charity. The alms houses were built in 1695 and maintained, its chaplains deriving income by offering a Gretna Green-style marriage licence. Funds were invested in land providing an income for the trust.

Today responsibility for the trust, now said to be one of the richest charities in England, lies with the Alderman of the City of London. Its scope has widened to include professional people in need of care as well as those in poverty for no fault of their own.

The manor was bought in 1711 by Sir Gregory Page, a man who had inherited huge wealth. His father had been a well to do brewer and traded beer with the government as investment in kind in the shares of the South Sea Company. By chance the father died leaving him 17,000 shares at four pence each and his shares were sold off at £500 each just before the famous bursting of the **South Sea Bubble**. The shares were at the peak of their value and Page netted £200,000 (nowadays millions) to make him the richest commoner in the land.

On Wricklemarsh he is said to have built a sumptuous mansion with a ballroom, an art gallery and 120 other rooms. The house stood at what is now the junction of Blackheath Park and Pond Rd. A print of the house is displayed at the entrance of Ranger's House. He landscaped the whole estate and employed such a huge number of staff that it is suggested that their quarters may have been the founding of Blackheath Village. But wealth didn't bring Page much happiness. His wife lived alone till she died at 76. Page had by then attempted to commit suicide several times. A grieving widower, Page proposed at the age of 84 to a Greenwich girl aged 20.

> *Page sent her a pair of white gloves accompanied by a note, "Take G from glove leaving love which I send to you." The scornful young lady replied, "Take P from Page which leaves age which don't suit."*

Page died a widower two years later. The estate was inherited by his nephew and sold off. Among the prospective buyers who visited the estate was **Clive of India**. The new owner, Cator, divided up the estate selling it in lots and the house was demolished in 1787.

Back on the heath at Morden College we turned left and came across one of the lots sold off of Wricklemarsh Estate. **The Paragon** was bought by John Cator and designed by **Michael Searles**. Searles created the present crescent shaped complex of seven blocks of 14 houses beautifully linked by a single storey colonnade. A masterpiece, it was started in 1794 but took 13 years to complete due to Searles's financial problems. Bombing in the 1939-45 war severely damaged some of the houses but gave the opportunity to C Bernard Brown to carry out sympathetic restoration eliminating some of the less attractive Victorian additions to the facade. The colonnades were made from coadestone – attributed to Eleanor Coade of Lambeth who introduced the cheaper artificial stone casting for finishing off castings such as the massive lions on display. The Royal Naval College makes plentiful use of coadestone.

Many Lord Mayors of London had rooms here as did a notorious 19th century couple. Two women, one of them dressed as a man are said to have lived here having moved in from Gloucester Circus. The 'lady' informed her acquaintances that she was about to marry a lord and visited the shops and artisans of the heath buying up a fabulous list of clothes, furniture and accessories. They disappeared with debts of £20,000. The interiors were fitted separately and are now apartments.

Other houses in South Row follow the line of the Paragon and define the present end of the heath together with St German's Place. Adjacent to the Paragon but on South Row is **Paragon House,** a pre-1796 Searles property once balanced off by another of his houses, Bryan House, which was destroyed during the war.

Turning left just before the Princess of Wales pub on Montpelier Row we came to **Colonnade House** on the right. Erected in 1806, it is another building believed to have been designed by Michael Searle.

We took Morden Rd to the left of Morden College and, at number 17, found the house which once housed Gounod, composer of the opera, *Faust.* Further down we came across a post box depicting the rare V.R. (Victoria Regina) insignia. We were on the way to Blackheath Park church built by Page Turner in the 18th century. The church's slender towering spire earned it the local name of the **Devil's Pick**. Less controversially, it was also known as the Needle of Kent. It was built as a chapel of ease where the incumbent cleric required worshippers to be pew paying customers and only became part of the Church of England in the early 1900s.

This part of the estate is speckled with some delightful old houses built by city merchants and offered an enjoyable stroll. One such property is the Gables opposite **Blackheath Concert Halls** (tel 0208 463 0100) on Lee Rd. The halls is one of south London's foremost music venues can be found on the right of Blackheath train station. Performances there range through poets, Thomas Thallis Music Society, Kent Opera, The Blues Band, Jools Holland, who resides in Blackheath, Tom Robinson and Children's Theatre.

The South Side of Blackheath

The top of Montpelier Vale brought us to the heath and in front of us, the beautiful spire of **All Saints Church**. The church was born in controversial circumstances, its siting illegally encroachming on the heath. Built in 1857 to the design of Benjamin Ferrey, it has a fascinating shape which, prior to the 1880s addition of the steeple, earned it the name of The Three Barns.

Terry Waite, the famous British hostage in the Lebanon, attended regularly before leaving for Beirut. As it was a Sunday morning, the service had begun. We tip-toed into the porch taking care to shut the door without making a noise. We peered through the glass door into the nave where the high church worshippers were gathered.

Unfortunately, we were spotted by an old woman, our efforts to remain inconspicuous were scuppered. We made a dignified retreat – that is until Muriel let the heavy latch slip with a bang which echoed thoughout the building. Visits are probably best arranged by contacting the warden.

Left from Montpelier Vale we came to the 18th century Georgian terraces of Montpelier Row. Just past Wemys Rd we came to a pair of purpose-built semi-detached houses built in the 1700s to a style which would become popular in the Victorian era. The 1970s Labour Prime Minister, **Jim Callaghan**, of whom one ministerial colleague said: "He suffers from what you may regard as a fatal defect in a Chancellor – he is always wrong," once occupied the modern house next door to the Clarendon Hotel.

The Clarendon Hotel

The two-star Clarendon Hotel sits in the middle of a row of historic buildings and offered a very comfortable stay. Close to the Meridian Line and situated on the heath, it has one of the finest locations in London. Once the home of wealthy Georgian merchants and shipbuilders, the building was partly constructed with stone from the old London Bridge. Thirty years ago the building comprised three hotels as part of the terrace: the Clarendon, the Regency and the Heathview, before being amalgamated into one by the current owners. In 1999 it celebrated its centenary as a guest house and hotel.

Previous guests here have included Brian Clough, one of Britain's greatest ever soccer managers. The hotel has frequently been used as a film location and guests have bumped into the comedian, Jasper Carrott, and cast members of the television series, *London's Burning* and *The Knock*.

We spent many a happy evening in the hotel's Chart Bar which echoes the area's maritime traditions with ancient and recent sea charts decorating the walls. The bar also boasts part of the stern from a queen's barge built for William of Orange in 1689. We didn't have a chance to go to the Clarendon's various theme nights (Mardi Gras nights, murder mysteries, psychic dinners etc.) or appreciate the restaurant dinner entertainment but other guests assured us they were great fun.

Guests are permitted free usage of a local private sports and leisure club, the lucky ones often invited by the manager, Ken, to join him when he goes rowing with the historic **Blackheath Rowing Club** at 7am. His staff are friendly and many are long-serving such as the 80-plus year old woman, a former *nippy* in Lyon's London tea houses who has worked at the hotel for thirty years.

Recently refurbished, the 200 rooms are virtually all *en suite*. With its siting, the hotel is very popular for holding functions. It also has an air-conditioned conference room able to seat 200 delegates.

Mike O'Donnell and members of the friendly family-owned hotel have created an excellent base for visitors wanting to explore the borough. The Clarendon (tel 0208 318 4321, fax 4378) is five minutes walk from Blackheath train station and a short bus ride from Greenwich. Rooms cost £79-£90 per night for a double which includes breakfast (£60- £70 for a single). There are also executive suites (£150 a double, £100 a single including breakfast) and a lovely honeymoon suite at £175 (flowers, fruit, champagne, chocolate and breakfast are included.) It is advised to book well in advance.

Further on is the **Princess of Wales pub** named after the heath socialite, Princess Caroline. It has a mixed crowd and the rich are said to dress down. The road leads onto South Row where one can find the Paragon.

Taking the left fork of the road from station, where Blackheath Vale begins, we found ourselves walking up **Tranquil Vale** – not so tranquil today with its numerous pubs and restaurants. The **Crown Inn** pub here dates back to the 1700s and rivals the former post office next door for being considered the oldest building in the village. The terraces from numbers 23 to 35 were bought by John Collins who in 1798 owned much of the west side of Blackheath. At number 34a, **Blackheath Gallery** (tel 0208 8521802) has a small art exhibition (open daily save Thursdays and Sundays between 10am and 6pm). We were now heading west to **Grotes Place** square and the fine buildings erected by **Andrew Grote** of Point House on Point Hill in the 1770s.

Although the properties had been developed for investment purposes, they nevertheless retained a sense of attractive individuality. The first, Lindsey House, has fine terraced houses while Grote was not responsible for the buildings at numbers 1-4 Grote's Place which are mid 19th century.

The area of The Orchard and Orchard Terrace edging the heath to Hare and Billet Rd was another encroachment, this time the 18th century work of Duncan Campbell who profited both from being overseer of the hulks prisonships moored in the Thames and from his slave plantation in Jamaica.

Proceeding on to the heath we arrived at Eliot Place, home to the Hare and Billet pond and the former cricketers' home, the Hare and Billet pub. Eliot Place contains an attractive row of buildings dating from the end of the 18th century. **Benjamin D'Israeli**, one of the foremost British Prime Ministers of the 19th century, spent some of his childhood being educated at a school which occupied what are now houses number 2 and 3. D'Israeli was the consummate politician, once remarking of his own party, "A Conservative government is an organised hypocrisy." He had many a parliamentary battle with the Liberal leader William Gladstone. One of his great quips to a heckler was: "Truth travels slowly but it will reach you in time."

Turning left before the next junction brought us into **Pagoda Gardens**, named after **The Pagoda** building, probably Blackheath's most lavish creation and similar to the Royal Pavilion in Brighton. It was constructed in the 1760s at the behest of the 4th Earl of Cardigan who lived at Rangers House. The Earl is believed to have wanted a summer house and when Princess Caroline moved into Montague House she used the Pagoda as her nursery school and garden. Moving on to Wat Tyler Rd at the most southerly part of the heath, we found **Dartmouth Row**, thought to have been another illegal encroachment on the heath.

Some of the houses on Dartmouth Row date back to the 1690s and as such are believed to have been the first residential developments on the heath. The crown claimed the land as belonging to the Royal Hundred of Greenwich but William Legge, then 2nd Baron Dartmouth and later **1st Earl of Dartmouth**, persuaded the government that it was part of the Manor of Lewisham.

The Earl created the family home at Dartmouth House, the large building to the south of the Church of Ascension. The church, built in 1697, functioned for two centuries as the Earls' private chapel. Today it is open to all for worship and also hosts **musical concerts** (tel 0208 852 5944). **Dartmouth House** was the manor house of Lewisham and later home to the religious College of Greyladies and later the Southwark Diocesan Home.

Up until 1689, numbers 21 and 23 were part of one mansion. After the 1812 assassination of prime minister Spencer Perceval, his family were linked with the house. Consequently the buildings are now known as Spencer House (number 23) and Perceval House (number 21). Number 18 Dartmouth Row was built in 1780 and once served as a post office

Ross, Polar Explorer and the North West Passage

A blue plaque on Ross House, at number 2 Eliot Place overlooking the heath declares: "Sir James Clark Ross 1800-1862 Polar Explorer lived here."

Ross was one of the great explorers of his time. In 1831 he discovered the magnetic north pole and later made several attempts to find the magnetic south pole. Over the Antarctic, his route was blocked by a 200ft wall of ice rising sheer from the sea, now known as the great Ross Ice Barrier, and the sea subsequently named the Ross Sea.

In an age when the idea of digging the Panama Canal was still not considered to be viable, another great quest was to find a sea route through North America to the Pacific and the

markets of the Far East. Ross's uncle, Sir John Ross, had been commissioned by the Admiralty in 1828 to discover the North West Passage as it was known. Uncle John took his nephew, James, along as midshipman on the unsuccessful expedition.

The voyage was to be the last the Admiralty were prepared to fund. The following year Sir John raised funds for a private expedition and again took James along, this time as second in command of the ship.

Plans for a two year trip went awry when their ship became ice bound for three years. It was during this period that James discovered the magnetic north pole. Sir John, James and crew took to sledges to continue and were eventually rescued when spotted by whalers.

In 1839 while in command of the ships, Erebus and Terror, James Ross set out on another polar quest this time to the Antarctic and the magnetic south pole. Ross made three trips becoming the first to circumnavigate the Antarctic continent and taking his ship to within 160 miles of the South Pole, further south than any explorer had ventured in known history. His route blocked again, he returned to England in 1843 where he eventually received a knighthood.

Though in love, Ross was prevented from marrying his sweetheart by her father until he pledged to give up his polar explorations. He relinquished and eventually married.

Sir John Franklin had set sail to discover the North West Passage in 1845. Nothing further had been seen of Franklin and his crew since being sighted in Baffin Bay in July of the same year. The Admiralty commissioned Sir James to lead an official search mission and he took along his Uncle John to assist. However, the mission was unsuccessful as were the many others that followed.

Almost a century later the bodies of Franklin and his crew were discovered. It is believed that they died of lead poisoning contracted from the lead tins used to store their food.

On his return from the Franklin quest Sir James was promoted to Rear Admiral, and died in Blackheath in 1862.

Montpelier Row, Blackheath

Life in Blackheath Village

The village buzzes with its range of fashionable shops. The 23 restaurants, the pubs and cafes pull in many visitors. During the day there are also some interesting places to visit including the **Age Exchange** (admission free) and its fascinating **Reminiscence Centre** (tel 0208 318 9105 e-mail: age-exchange@lewisham.gov.uk). Crossing the road from **Blackheath Railway Station** we turned right, climbed the slope and arrived within two minutes.

Age Exchange was set up to improve the lives of the elderly by stressing the worth of their memories to old and young alike. Activities include recording and displaying old people's memories, artistic creation, youth theatre, education, welfare, computer courses, and showing classic films. The Reminiscence Centre, with its professional **theatre group,** encourages old people to enjoy their memories. While schools use the centre, the Exchange is more than glad to welcome senior citizens from around the world in groups or individually. There is also a bookshop. Opening times are daily 10am-5.50pm, closed Sundays. The centre can be reached by train or the 54, 89, 108, 202, 306 and 853 buses which all stop outside the centre.

As we entered we were whisked back into the 1930s. The shop contained an array of household items from the pre-war period which included sealing wax, hats and gloves, a wind-up gramophone, wartime gas masks and ration books. The past was displayed in such profusion that the whole effect conjured up images of those inter-war black and white films. Had it not been for the silent 90s music box used to play CDs, it was easy to believe that we'd just jumped out of a Tardis and found ourselves back 60 years.

A few steps led us into the centre. Those with disabilities are invited to use the wheelchair lift. Above the main counter we eyed a pulley system once used in department stores to carry money on overhead rope cables to the cashiers' office.

The next room played host to an exhibition of life for children in the wartime evacuation and to the rear in the theatre room elderly volunteers were stuffing envelopes and talking about their wartime experiences in the East End. In between the two rooms is a rock garden popular for those wishing to relax, bringing out their drinks from the **cafeteria**.

A new and exciting jazz venue is the ***Green Club*** (tel 0208 852 0883) at the Cactus Pit, where the legendary jazz musician Brian Green has been playing. To the right, and on the same side as the train station, is Lawn Terrace, housing Blackheath's most popular swanky restaurant. ***Lawn*** (0208 355 0111) was re-launched in 1999 by the former team at the award-winning Bank Restaurant and Bar. The five star team is headed by Frenchman Christian Delteil who at Bank won every restaurant award worth winning.

Up on the first floor we found a bright minimalist eating area. Exposed beams, pipes and light wooden floors make it a very modern design. Comfort is not abandoned and stone-coloured fabrics cover the relaxing chairs. The fayre can again be described as modern English international. Starter prices range from £4 to £8.50 for the smoked salmon and horseradish cream. Main course begin at £10 and go to £15.50 for grilled rib eye, bearnaise sauce and fat chips. There are plenty of wines to choose from, beginning at £14 a bottle and rising to £139 for two bottles of *Cote Rotie, La Mouline*.

The Lawn's ground floor has a new wine and cocktail bar open to non diners who can listen to the variety of jazz artists from Chelsea's 606 club entertaining every Monday from 8pm. Opening hours are noon to 2.30pm and 6pm – 11pm, Tuesdays to Fridays and 6-11pm Saturdays. The restaurant has 150 seats, disability access and baby changing facilities.

We came back to the ***Fairway and Firkin pub*** beside the train station for a cheaper lunch. One of the more stylish Firkin pubs and popular with the under 40s, it has a good selection of real ales, televised sports coverage and music nights. Food is available all day, ranging from £2.50 to £5, and proved a filling lunch. Once known as the Railway Hotel, the building has been a pub since 1851. In 1975 it must have set a record when it achieved its 51st year of retaining the same landlady.

We walked left from the station up Montpelier Vale and noted the busy French run ***Cafe Rouge*** where we would return for an excellent espresso. Opposite at numbers 7-9 was **Cave Austin** (tel 0208 297 2847) We visited the sixties-style elegant bar on several evenings. Drinks are expensive but the age is mixed, and the atmosphere chic but friendly. The restaurant serves a good variety of modern English international dishes and at the rear has a lovely Japanese garden.

Further along at numbers 43-45 is the new, modern **Chapter Two** (tel 0208 333 2666) restaurant, sister to the award-winning Chapter One close to Bromley. With chef John Wood from the famous Dorchester Hotel and Adrian Jones it has set out to be the premier restaurant of the 23 currently available in the village. John Wood's style has been described as ranging from, 'serious classic' to 'modern European cooking'. The restaurant is open from noon till 2.30pm daily, 6.30pm-10.30pm Mon-Thurs, 6.30pm-11pm Sat and 7pm-9.30pm, Sun.

BLACKHEATH

Blackheath Royal Standard

Turning right from Montpelier Vale along Montpelier Row, the road becomes Prince of Wales Rd which leads up to the other centre of Blackheath, a busy area centred by a green and known as Blackheath Royal Standard. Located aroung the green are shops and the Royal Standard traditional English pub with a **pool table** and **darts** games, giving the area its name. A Barclay's bank sits opposite the pub and across the green is a Chinese restaurant and Gambardella's Cafe.

We took the 108 bus to the Standard. Now a less salubrious part of Blackheath, it nevertheless contains one particular gem, the house of **Woodlands** at 90, Mycenae Rd. Entering Woodlands we were struck by the elegant mosaic on the step beneath the columned portal. The mosaic has existed since 1774 when John Julius Angerstein ordered the building of the house.

Angerstein had married and built Woodlands as a healthy retreat from his house Pall Mall house in the busy city. He installed a central heating system of hot air flues. The house was guest to many a royal visitor including **George III** and Princess Caroline. Other visitors included Dr Samuel Johnson and his friend **Sir Thomas Lawrence** whose portrait of Angerstein hangs in the National Gallery.

Today the house is home to **Woodlands Art Gallery** on the ground floor and **Greenwich Local History Library** on the first floor. Opposite the gallery reception we entered the area formerly used as a drawing room by John Julius. Much has changed and the house was taken over by nuns for a long period. Up above we could see the decorative mould of the original ceiling. The doorways are also original. To the rear of the building one can easliy imagine the attractive views which John Julius must have enjoyed of the grounds, stretching all the way down to the Thames. Today, although the grounds are much reduced they once included a lake, an ice house and a large heated conservatory. Nevertheless the grounds retain almost 100 species of wild flowers and trees.

John Julius Angerstein

John Julius Angerstein, was the founder of Lloyd's and first contributor to the National Gallery. Believed to have been born in 1735, John Julius Angerstein's parents remain a point of dispute. He is thought to have been an illegitimate son of Elizabeth, Empress of Russia, herself the illegitimate daughter of Peter the Great. At 14 years old, Angerstein was sent to England to learn his trade in a London merchant banking house.

He became a leading shipping insurer at the famous marine insurance institution, Lloyd's. In 1770 Lloyds hit a crisis. Many of the brokers and insurers were mere gamblers and the principal brokers and insurers broke away. Determined to build a more stable and reputable institution, 79 of them set up a new Lloyd's Coffee House at Pope's Head Alley.

Angerstein was a leading member and between 1790 and 1796 was continually appointed chairman. Among his friends was Britain's youngest ever Prime Minister, William Pitt. Under his stewardship Lloyds gave financial support to sailors killed in the wars against revolutionary France at the Battle of the Nile and the Battle of Copenhagen.

After the Battle of Copenhagen, Horatio Nelson wrote to Angerstein, "I feel - and I am certain every man in the fleet does the same – much indebted to the Gentlemen of the Committee for the attention they pay and trouble they experience on this occasion." The letter is now exhibited in the Nelson Room at Lloyd's.

Amongst Angerstein's friends were King George III and his notorious daughter-in-law, Princess Caroline. The artist Thomas Lawrence was also a friend and credited with having an affair with the princess while she was married to George, Prince of Wales. The gossip of the time declared that Lawrence was the father of Caroline's illegitimate son, William Austin.

Angerstein was an enthusiastic patron of the arts. His first purchase was The Rape of the Sabines by Rubens, and he went on to buy many more including works by Rembrandt, Velasquez, Titian, Raphael and Correggio. He also collected Hogarth paintings and early drawings by the young Turner

BLACKHEATH

who would become Britain's most renown artist. On his death in 1823, the paintings were due to be sold to the Prince of Orange when the government in the form of Lord Liverpool stepped in and bought the collection.

The Angerstein acquisition formed the nucleus of the National Gallery and inspired others to contribute. His collection now in the gallery includes works by Carraci, Correggio, Raphael, Titian, Claude, Poussin, Rembrandt, Rubens, Vandyke and Hogarth. Until the National Gallery was built in Trafalgar Square the portraits were hung for public view in Angerstein's former home in Pall Mall. Angerstein was buried at St Alfege Church in Greenwich where there is a memorial tablet to him and his family.

Woodlands Art Gallery (tel 0208 858 5847) has 10 showings a year. Opening hours are Mon to Sat 11am –5pm, Sun 2pm-5pm and closed Wednesdays. Up the stairs **Greenwich Local History Library** (tel 0208 858 4631 fax 293 4721) has a huge collection of works featuring Greenwich and we found a friendly staff keen to help us find out all we needed to know about the area. The collection of borough material dates back to 1387. The library also holds local water colours and sketches dating back to the 1760's and sketchbooks by Caroline Angerstein. Photocopying and colour laser copying facilities are available. Group visits are welcome by prior notice and talks can be arranged.

The library opens at 9am on Mon, Tues, Thurs and Sat. Closing times are 5.30pm Mon, Tues, 8pm Thurs and 5pm Sat. With no lifts, neither the steps, stairs or toilets are adapted for disabled access though staff will help and guide dogs are welcome. Smoking, eating and drinking in the library are not permitted. Refreshments are available in the community centre next door.

The Village, Blackheath

SHOOTERS HILL **and its Ancient Woods**

We set off from Blackheath up Shooters Hill Road (A207) at the summit of which is the infamous hill. Along the way, we came across the site of a former army barracks on the left and on the right, another old military building, the Royal Herbert Hospital. Built in 1865, and surrounded by 20 acres of land it was designed by Sir Douglas Galton, government Under Secretary of War and nephew to Florence Nightingale. Fashioned in yellow brick with stone dressings in the Italianate/Byzantine style, it was the first in Britain to be built on the Pavilion principle. Separate wards were connected by a long corridor with pavilions attached at intervals. The hospital had space for 650 beds. Today it is known as the Royal Herbert Pavilions and retaining its former splendour, it has been converted into private residential apartments.

We stopped at Ankerdine Crescent on the hill. It's a quiet road with a splendid view across London and the Dome. Moving on, we arrived at Eagles Field, the common on the very top of Shooters Hill, a huge area of London clay elevated into the mound. From here there are clear views south across acres of woodland over to the Kent Downs. From the other side of the hill we had magnificent views across to Essex, the Chilterns, and down the Thames Valley. In the past the hill served an important strategic purpose, giving whoever controlled the hill plenty of warning of approaching traffic, friend or foe.

The hill was therefore a key point on the London to Dover road, the Roman Watling Road and the Pilgrims' Way to Canterbury in the Middle Ages. At night the summit of the hill offers a view east of house-lights stretching to Dover. A track is said to have preceded the Romans, possibly as a route for the local tribes such as the chariot riding Belgi, centred on Colchester. A mound in Plum Lane which has never been excavated is thought to be either an ancient burial ground dating back to the Bronze Age.

The top of the hill was probably an ancient feeding station and the left side of the road still has the Roman foundations. Many Roman and mediaeval relics were found here, some of which can be seen in Plumstead Museum. The surrounding woods and valleys also testify to the area being a profitable location for highwaymen who could leap out of bushes, making good their escape via the numerous highways proffered by the forest. As early as 1215 the forests were said to harbour a, "nest of highway robbers" threatening merchants and pilgrims alike. In 1313 during the reign of Edward II a royal order proclaimed that the highway on 'Shoters Held' be enlarged, the hill being described as a fearful place for travellers.

The Highwaymen and Highwaywomen of Shooters Hill

Newspaper reports of highway robberies at the Blackheath end of Shooters Hill were frequent. Dick Turpin, the famous highway robber, is said by some to have frequented the hill. These rumours were disputed but a 1735 newspaper reported that "for about six weeks past Blackheath has been so infested by two highwaymen (supposed to be Rowden [the Pewterer] and Richard Turpin) that tis dangerous for travellers to pass". Legend has it that Dick's mistress, Fanny, would wave a lamp at night to warn the villain of approaching officers of the law. She even has a local pub named after her, The Fanny on the Hill in East Wickham.

In the 1740s the woods were the stalking ground for the notorious robber, Claude Duval. The son of a Camberwell butcher, Duval claimed his father was a French nobleman, and was hung in 1752. However, not all the brigands were men. In 1719 one particular report stated how three women with pistols had set upon a manservant , forced him off his horse and left him 100 guineas the lighter. Many of the highway robbers were vicious bandits but reports of the day also mentioned more gentlemanly robbers of the time.

In 1752 one man was robbed at gun point and reported that the highwayman "asked the gentleman's pardon and said that he was drove to this through the treacherous and cruel usage he met with from a near relation, who reduced him to this extremity." Other reports comment on robbers being polite, shaking hands with their victims and bidding them goodnight. Amongst those robbed were Sir Gregory Page of Wricklemarsh Manor, Mr Angerstein of Woodlands, Blackheath and a Mr Bennett, Treasurer of Morden College. By 1800 50 coaches with armed passengers were passing over the hill each day and in 1810 a plan was even developed to dig a tunnel beneath the hill to avoid the bands of muggers. When Princess Charlotte stayed at Shrewsbury House, armed escorts were still being provided to take guests from the Sun in the Sands to houses on the hill. Highwaymen eventually fell out of fashion and were replaced by gangs extorting protection money from travellers.

SHOOTERS HILL

Shooters Hill

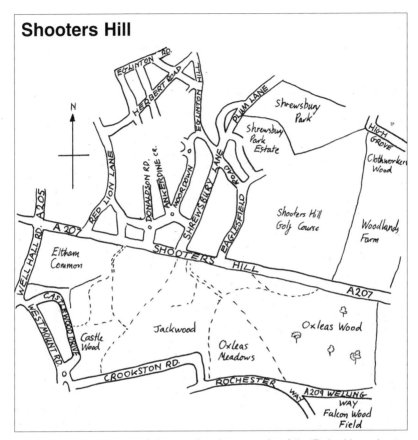

The hill was once part of the vast hunting grounds of the Tudor kings due to its proximity to Eltham Palace. **Oxleas Wood** is the principal wood, the others being **Jack Wood, Castle Wood** and **Eltham Common.** Eagles Fields is not an allusion to hunting. The Lidgburd family (having built a successful business providing bricks for local buildings) once owned the tops of the hill. The family crest displayed bricks and an eagle, hence the common became known as Eagles Field. Likewise, the name Shooters Hill did not originate from hunting nor, since the name originated at least as early as 1313, or from the presence of highway men and women. In fact it is believed to have earned its name due to the popularity of the site for practising archers.

In the first chapter of *Tale of Two Cities*, Dickens wrote of a journey up the terrible Shooters Hill, and Byron mentioned the hill in a poem. A great fictional character who travelled up this hill was Defoe's Roxana on her way from the Minnories in London to Dover.

Just below the north side of the hill, hidden in woodland was the Upper Gibbets Field and the golf course was once Lower Gibbets Field. After being hanged the dead were transferred to a gibbet. These are the fields where the famous diarist, **Samuel Pepys**, saw corpses hanging, many of them highwaymen from the woods. In 1661 he wrote: "Mrs Anne and I rode under the man that hangs upon Shooters Hill, and a filthy sight it was to see how his flesh is sunk to the bones."

Beyond the golf course is the site of the last farm in London. Woodlands Farm covers 89 acres and was established at least 150 years ago when Bushy Lees Wood was cleared. The farmhouse dates to 1890 and is now being restored. It will be available for visits in the future as part of the nature reserve. Adjacent to the farm is the small Clothworkers Wood, ancient woodland which was then used by the farm as the bloody site of the abattoir. (Woodland Farm Trust can be phoned on 0208 319 8900. Buses 89 and 178 go along the A207 road on Shooters Hill and stop outside the entrance)

SHOOTERS HILL

Shrewsbury House in Shrewsbury Park sits on the Plumstead side of Shooters Hill. The original late 18th century house was built by the Earl of Shrewsbury and later served as a residence of Princess Caroline her temporary move to the Old Rectory House in Charlton and then on to Montague House in Blackheath. On the princess' departure, it was leased to the Crown for use by her and George IV's only daughter, Princess Charlotte.

The house was sold off and saw use as a boarding school and a convalescent home for sick children, before being demolished in 1923 to make way for the current building, a community centre and library. Close by is **Rose Cottage**, the sole survivor of the 18th century cottages built for the upper servants. Princess Charlotte's tutor, Dr Watson, lived there and readily admitted to paying protection money to the brigands controlling the route over Shooters Hill. In 1800, he is said to have sent the first electrical signals over the Thames and back – decades ahead of Marconi. The house today is known as **Prospect House**.

The forest looking south is the beautiful **Oxleas Wood** with its woodlands dating back 8,000 years. It can be entered by taking the road to the right opposite the large water tower at the top of the hill. The main car park (open 9am-6pm) for the woods is close to Oxleas meadow, a vast field which rolls down the hill with **Castle Wood** to the left.

The pavilion at the top of the meadow holds a cafe here where one can sample inexpensive, basic food and sit outside. (Open daily, winter 9.30am-3.30pm, summer 9.30am-6pm). The menu is limited but the food good and costs anything from £1.50 to £4. The cafe and car park can be reached by turning off Shooters Hill Rd into Kenilworth Gardens and taking the two left forks. The cafe also offers beautiful views of the woods, Kent and the south. For more details of walks, contact the **Green Chain Office** (0208 312 5884).

The green open space contains a large variety of grasses and is surrounded by woods and popular at weekends during the summer. To the right from the cafe, a maze of paths takes one through the woods full of ancient oaks, ash, silver birch and beeches, many twisting and curling and festooned with creepers. It seemed as if we'd stumbled into an enchanted wood of fantasies, shafts of sunlight lighting our way.

These woods contain some of Britain's most ancient trees including Midland hawthorn and wild service varieties, which are only found in the oldest of woods. Then there are hornbeams, aspens, geans, rowans, mature wild cherry and alders. Beneath were smatterings of sweet chestnut, hazel, field, maple, guelder rose and dogthorn challenging the foreign intruders, rhododendrons, cherry laurel and conifers.

In the spring there would be blue-purple fields of bluebells separating the bramble and bracken. Wild angelica and yellow pimpernel hide in the grassland and compete with the 200 species of macro-fungi for being the wood's most remarkable flora. Occasionally it's possible to see pheasants, woodcocks, brambling and chipping woodpeckers. Stalking the wood are hedgehogs, rabbits, foxes, badgers and grey squirrel. Above fly nuthatch birds, jays, tree creepers, chiffchaff, spotted flycatchers, magpies and tawny owls.

Soon we came across the ruins of **Castle Wood House**, set above a crocus-strewn grass bank and reached by steps. We initially mistook this old building for **Severndroog Castle** for which we had gone in search. Pretty as the ruins of Castle Wood House are, they represent just the rose garden terrace of the house behind which was pulled down to increase the open spaces. We were eventually told that Severndroog was further on and up the hill to the right. The path twisted and forked as the London roar of car engines filtered away to be replaced by the twittering of birds and humming of insects. Passing through patches of spring mud we finally climbed the hill to see the old castle appearing through the tops of the trees.

It's easy to see why the castle built in 1784, is known as Lady Jane's Folly.

The Gothic tower is around 60ft high with each side around 20ft long. Battlemented at the top with towers at each corner, it has a series of windows for each floor and appears more like a tower occupied by a damsel in distress. The architect, **Richard Jupp**, also designed the front of Guy's Hospital in London.

Lady Jane's husband, **Sir William James** led the troops from his East India Company ships to storm the fortress island of Janjeera Soowumdroog off the coast of Malabar (now Kerala, south India) in 1755. He successfully defeated the pirates of Cona Agrea capturing a thousand, and freed the Kerala coast for trading. James also relieved Clive of India's troops under siege in the Indian town of Chandanagore and on his return to the UK captured a French fleet carrying arms and ammunition to India. Retiring to Park Place, Eltham, he died at 67 during his daughter's wedding. Lady Jane built the castle in his memory. Clive became the great celebrated conqueror of India.

SHOOTERS HILL

The first matter we wanted to check was whether the castle was three or four sided. We met a woman from Manchester who was stood waiting for her husband. "He's walking round the tower, " she said in a Mancunian accent. "I told him there are only three sides but he insists there are four. I told him that he had counted the first turret twice when he walked round but he won't believe me. Now he's put a ketchup packet on the ground to mark his start and he's going round again." Her husband returned chastened and thankful he hadn't wagered any money on his convictions.

The castle was requisitioned by the army as an observation post. It is said that one can see seven counties from its top. Sadly this view is seldom possible as it is rarely open to the public. The quickest way to get to Severndroog Castle is to follow the path below Craigholme on the south east side of Shooters Hill Rd. In Jackwood only the wall fountain and the terraced gardens remain of the great Jackwood House. The Lodge at the entrance to the wood was built in the late 19th century as two cottages forming the stables and staff quarters for Jackwood House.

East of the castle lies Eltham Common with a similar woodland population, but including wild pear, crab apple, hazel and beneath, the rare common cow wheat.

Moving on we came to **Telegraph Field** on the other peak on Shooters Hill. Its name says it all. The hill was an important location used for communication by fire and telegraph during the Napoleonic wars, then later by Morse transmission. Some consider that as early as Saxon times the hill was used for beacon fires. Edward III is also thought to have used the hill as part of a system of bonfires. He later had tall poles erected with iron cages on top in which a fire would be lit.

An inn called The Catherine Wheel once stood at the site of the Memorial Home, across the road from a 15th century beacon site. Said to be part of a

Severndroog Castle

chain of hilltop beacons stretching to Deal and Dover, it was maintained by the Parish of Eltham who manned it round the clock. It would certainly have been used in 1688 to warn of the Armada's approaching ships.

In the mid 18th century, the beacon was replaced with a telegraph manned by the military whereby coded messages were sent to distant locations. Two men operated the equipment while two others manned the telescopes searching for the signals from other stations. It was now possible for a signal sent from Dover to arrive in London within two minutes.

As life became safer on the hill in the early 19th century, the rich began to settle on its steeps which offer views of the Thames. Telegraph Hill was 460 feet above sea level but now stands at 415 feet. However, this was not because of the sinking South East. The hill was too steep and horses had to be changed at the bottom of the hill if carriages were too make the peak. The Turnpike Trust brought in labour to lower the hill and so reduce the gradient producing a less strenuous incline. The excavated gravel was taken used for roads and pathways. Hence the riddle, "Where is the top of Shooters Hill". On the other side of the hill, still on Shooters Road, we came to **The Old Bull,** close to where once stood a public house of the same name said to be the grandest in the land.

Opposite the Catherine Wheel, The Bull was the second pub to be built on top of the hill. The Bull became a very popular dining place for the rich. The pub was described by **William Hickey** in 1761 as, "out and out the most expensive tavern in all England, where however you will be served in a princely style and find every article of the best."

Very expensive, it catered for the highest ranking officers at **Woolwich Barracks** and the **Arsenal**. So many officers frequented the pub that an unofficial officers' mess was established. In 1785 one newspaper reported on eight gentlemen from the city who, having visited the Bull for a party, were robbed on their way home. The pub also became a popular place for annual balls, adversely affecting the Catherine Wheel's trade which completely fell away resulting in its closure.

By 1810, Woolwich Artillery Barracks had its own officers' mess and the Bull declined in popularity becoming more of a drinking house. In 1888 it was demolished and replaced by the current pub of the same name. Today's pub, a Courage house, is said to have a ghost, that of an ex-landlady who is said to walk the corridors in a grey dress. The current landlady said she had never seen it and suggested that the ghost' might be her husband in drag.

It's a traditional pub, with a dart board and television in the public bar and prints of stagecoaches and huntsmen adorning the walls of the saloon bar. A door in the saloon bar leads to a turfed and well kept beer garden. A pleasant place to stop for a drink after a stroll in the woods.

SHOOTERS HILL

Nearby, at the side of the road opposite Kenilworth Gardens and the entrance to the woods, we saw the **Mounting Stone**, a step used for climbing into the stagecoaches which ran along the route. Older than the Bull, it was probably used by the pub's thirsty travellers. We puzzled over the tall brick tower which stands close by without a hint of its past or duties. In fact it is the grade 2 listed **Water Tower**, built in 1910. Its walls enclose a 75ft high, 25ft diameter steel tank taking water pumped up from chalk wells at Orpington. The water is then allowed to fall by gravity along pipes to a pumping station on Well Hall Rd in Eltham.

Opposite is the two storey Georgian house, **Holbrooke**. Built in 1790 it was altered in 1862 by **Hayden Maynard**, architect of London's Charing Cross station.

From there we moved on to the north or London side of Shooters Hill looking down on the former Royal Academy and central London. The purging wells here, once part of a health spa, were expected to rival Bath in South West England. However the Napoleonic Wars intervened and the hills use as a military centre ended the challenge.

Further down the hill we came to flats at the junction where Shooters Hill meets Academy Rd and Well Hall Rd. On the left the police station lamp still stands. Shooters Hill had a police station and a police force much earlier than most areas. The site no longer has a police station and, fortunately, is no longer a hanging ground for the numerous gruesome public hangings once staged here. Fox and Russell, betrayed by their gang, were sentenced to die in the last multiple hanging. They were hanged there in 1803 near the Fox under the Hill pub. The military had to turn out to control the thousands who attended and the Fox did a great trade. The dead were transferred to the Gibbets Fields before finally being buried beside the police station.

Top: Greenwich Market. *Bottom left* The Village Market. *Bottom right:* The Cutty Sark.

Queen's House

Top: Queen's House colonnade. *Bottom:* Deer in Greenwich Royal Park.

Streets and parks of Greenwich

General Wolf, Greenwich Royal Park.

Top: Eltham Palace. *Bottom:* Boats for hire, Greenwich Royal Park.

Top: Kites on the heath. *Bottom:* Blackheath Village streets.

Clockwise from top left: Eltham Palace: in the Courtaulds' Building; Virginia Courtauld's bathroom; Eltham Palace in winter; looking into the Courtauld's dining room (interior photos Jonathan Bailey, all photos courtesy of English Heritage).

Top: Cannon at the Artillery's Rotunda Museum. *Bottom:* Cannon barrels at the Rotunda Museum

The Royal Artillery Barracks and Parade Ground.

Clockwise from top: St Nicholas Church, Plumstead; Oxleas Wood; Lesnes Abbey ruins.

Clockwise from top: the Thames Barrier; Thamesmead; Southmere Lake.

Top: Arriving at the Millennium Dome. *Bottom:* North Greenwich underground station.

Top: The Dome's roof structure. *Bottom:* The Dome with Canary Wharf Tower.

ELTHAM'S **Parks and Palaces**

Records relate that the Saxon lord Alwold held the rich Manor of Eltham and, as he was more than likely a Christian, had a church built on what is now St Johns. He was followed around 1066 at the time of the Norman Conquest by Duke Haimo who numbered in his property nine slaves. William the Conqueror had arrived from Normandy with his armies in 1066, defeating the English king, **Harold**, and occupying the whole of England.

Haimo, a relation of William and Odo, took over Alwold's manor and was made, as Shire reeve (Sheriff) of Kent, the king's representative in the county. Odo, William's half brother, plotted against the king. Haimo joined in the conspiracy but survived William's wrath when the plot was discovered. The Earls of Gloucester later resided at Eltham till their particular lineage died out and the real story of the palace began in 1293 when a William de Vesci traded land in the Midlands in order to gain the estate. De Vesci died soon after, and with no legitimate heirs, he willed **Eltham Palace** to his illegitimate son, also named William de Vesci.

But parents could not legally pass on wealth to illegitimates. Instead, de Vesci used an 'enfeoffment' to Bishop Bec of Durham whereby the Bishop rented the land for the payment of one sparrow hawk a year. The Bishop was then expected to hand over the land to the young de Vesci.

However, de Vesci never got his hands on the property. Possessing powerful friends, Bec was able to build a moated manor house with half a dozen towers where the current palace now stands. By 1297, **King Edward I** was a guest at Eltham. He returned in 1299 and, from here, issued his proclamation against the people of Scotland. So powerful was Bec that when he joined the king to fight against the Scottish at the Battle of Falkirk, he was able to field his own private army which was bigger than the king's.

Fearing Bec's power, Edward tried to divest the Bishop of his Durham lands, prompting Bec to travel to Rome to petition the Pope. Edward replied by declaring that the Bishop was stripped of all his property. The king eventually relented to appease the Pope. Bec was forced to do penance before being restored to his bishopric. The king, being at odds with the Prince of Wales, is said to have given Eltham to him, following Bec's death in 1311. The outer walls of Bec's manor are still visible.

The Prince of Wales moved in and having been crowned Edward II, had his bride-to-be, Isabella the Fair, stay at Eltham before she made her royal entry into London. The regal couple often stayed at Eltham and their second son, **Prince**

Eltham

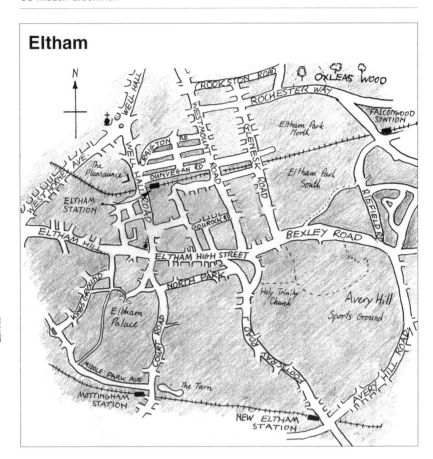

John of Eltham was born in the palace's Royal Chapel.

Isabella eventually deserted her husband, and from Eltham supported the claims of her sons to the throne. Revolts broke out against Edward and the people of London rose up for Prince John, capturing the Tower of London where the prince was staying. Edward II was captured and imprisoned at Berkeley Castle in Gloucestershire. But it was Isabella's first son who replaced Edward II and was crowned Edward III in 1327. John was made Earl of Cornwall.

While Edward was away fighting, John deputised as Prince Regent. He enlarged Eltham palace and records show that three builders who successfully tendered for the job by using cheap mortar, caused the walls to fall down. The 14th century 'cowboys' were forced to replace them at their own expense.

Prince John of Eltham

Prince John was one of the few royals to be born and baptised at Eltham Palace. At the tender age of three his father, King Edward II declared that he should have his income from all the Scottish men who lived south of the River Trent. Even then it amounted to a considerable sum of money.

When John's brother ascended the throne in 1327, England was in turmoil, wars being fought at home and abroad. By 1329, his brother was away in France and at 13 years old, John was appointed Prince Regent and thus temporary ruler of England. The same would happen in 1331 and 1332. John spent much of his time at Eltham with his mother Isabella.

In 1333 it was John's turn to travel when he commanded part of the English army that defeated the Scottish at Halidon Hill. Two years later headed another army that defeated the Scottish. Edward returned to London leaving the Prince in charge. However disease was rife in the British camp and John was taken sick, dying in Perth in 1336. Only 20 years old, he was buried at Westminster Abbey.

His brother the king, escorted his body to the abbey where a white marble monument was built showing John in his armour and coronet. It can be seen in St Edmund's Chapel. Unfortunately, a canopy erected above the monument collapsed under the weight of mourners who used it as a makeshift gallery in 1776. Today Eltham observes the tradition whereby children lay red roses on John's tomb on the anniversary of his death.

The moat walls were built and in the same year, Horn Park, Middle Park and the Great Park land on the estate were walled. The walls stretched from what is now Court Rd to Chislehurst and Lee Green and back to the palace. We visited the parts of the walls that still exist in Court Yard and Kings Park. The public were once forbidden from entering and did so on pain of death.

Edward III lived much longer, moving into the palace and rebuilding the kitchens. The Great Hall and the apartments were rebuilt using Kentish and Reigate stone quarried in the Medway area. The stone was shipped up the Thames to be offloaded at Woolwich. Peasant labour was conscripted at a half-penny a day (plus bread and cheese) to shift the stone on rollers and sleds to Eltham. For timber, rather than cut trees from his hunting grounds, Edward sent

Prince John of Eltham

lumberjacks out to cull trees in forest tracts owned by the church.

To the left as one enters Court Yard, one can see the large walls behind which lies the empty arena known as the **Tilt Yard**. Here Edward III would hold jousting competitions which would attract up to 20,000 people including foreign kings, dukes, knights, courtiers and their huge retinue. Here, knights in armour and often on horseback with long lances would challenge each other to prove their skill and valour. In 1354 this form of martial arts attracted the king's son, Edward, known as the **Black Prince** to fight.

It was **Edward III** who founded the **Order of the Garter,** one of the most prestigious royal awards in Britain. Today it is awarded for service to the monarch, and is said to have originated from the legends of King Arthur's Knights of the Round Table. The first award was made at Eltham's Grand Joust in 1347. Twelve Garters embroidered with the motto "*Honi soi qui mal y pense*" were given to the highest ranking of nobles sworn to serve the king.

The king was in need of much support for he was beset by problems. During the same year, Edward was forced to issue a decree from Eltham to deal with the prevalence of counterfeit English coinage which had brought the king's currency into disrepute throughout Europe. In 1355 Parliament petitioned that the Black Prince should be made Prince of Wales but the king refused. He now faced the possibility of going to war with France which would lead to Eltham Palace becoming the home of the French King, **John Le Bon.**

The occasion was the **Battle of Poitiers** in 1356. The French army would face the same fate as Napoleon faced at Waterloo, the English weather. Napoleon's heavy artillery was bogged down in heavy mud. At Poitiers the heavily armoured

French knights at the bottom of the hill also became stuck in the mud, and were slaughtered by English troops encamped on the hill. It is said that most of the French aristocracy was captured or slain.

King John II of France (King John Le Bon) was one of the captives. Held for ransom, he was taken to England and incarcerated in Eltham Palace for four years. But his treatment was not that onerous. He was lavishly entertained at the palace while the annual ransom of 33 pence was paid for four years. The French king was released after payment of the first instalment and his two sons kept as hostage.

The chivalrous code of the time allowed for hostages to return home to raise their ransoms. One such hostage reneged on his promise. John Le Bon was said to be so infuriated that he offered himself as hostage and returned to Eltham for another happy seven years. Many is the ballad that was composed of the French king's actions.

The Black Prince died before Edward, therefore it was **Richard II** who assumed the throne on Edward's death in 1377. Richard also lived in the palace while it underwent numerous improvements. The drawbridge over the moat was replaced with the current bridge and another bridge, which still stands, was built at the rear. They are known to be the oldest bridges in London.

Chaucer was made Clerk of the Works at the palace. On a single day in 1387, charged with taking the staff wages to the palace, he was robbed of the £10 in his possession three times while passing through south London. On the final occasion he had borrowed the money from his wife. Pleading to the king, he was eventually absolved of his debt by a writ from Richard II.

The Houses of Lancaster and York

The kings Henry were called Lancastrians and the kings Edward, Yorkists. The Lancastrians used Eltham as their holiday palace.

In 1398 Richard had himself declared absolute monarch at a parliament con- vened in Richmond. He then banished all those relations who he suspected of plotting against him. However in 1399, his cousin Henry Bolingbroke returned to England, defeated Richard and had him killed. The son of John of Gaunt, Bolingbroke assumed power for the House of Lancaster as King Henry IV.

By 1401 Henry IV felt secure enough to defortify Eltham Palace and many other castles. The narrow slit windows were replaced with large glass windows. However in 1404 the Duke of York broke into the palace with the intention of assassinating Henry. He was caught and put to death. Henry died in 1413 and was succeeded by **Henry V** who immediately went off to fight at the celebrated **Battle of Agincourt**. His prisoners were taken back to Eltham Palace before he went off to be greeted by the Lord Mayor of London on Blackheath.

Henry V died in 1422 and was replaced by his infant son, Henry VI. As he was only nine months old, the Duke of Exeter was made Protector of the Infant King in the former king's will. The Duke of Bedford was made Regent of France and the Duke of Gloucester was made Regent of England. This angered members of the Beaufort dynasty (led by the Bishop of Winchester) who were excluded from the highest counsel of the land.

At 21, the pious withdrawn Henry married the 15 year old Margaret of Anjou. Iron-willed, she is said to have built her own section of the palace to suit herself. Queen Margaret was also said to have provoked the War of the Roses which was actually a battle for succession between the Red Rose of the House of Lancaster and the White Rose of the House of York.

During the struggle for power, Henry was finally captured and imprisoned, for the most part, at Eltham Palace. He was eventually taken to the Tower of London and executed in 1471. The House of York installed the 19 year-old Edward IV to the throne. He and his wife lived at Eltham and in an attempt to ingratiate the House of Lancaster, invited them to many of his lavish functions.

The Palace shopping list for the 2,000 guests invited for Christmas 1482 read: 1,000 sheep, 1,000 geese, 2,400 quail, 2,000 capon, 1,500 hot venison pasties, 1,000 cold venison pasties, 304 calves and six bulls.

To accommodate these huge functions Edward had the Great Hall built on the site of the demolished Great Chamber. Quality Reigate stone was used for the façade, while cheaper ragstone was used to the rear. The hammerbeam style roof, made from chestnut wood reinforced with iron spikes, was one of the earliest in the country and remains of the finest and largest in the land. It also offered an efficient means of removing smoke from the open fires lit to accommodate the guests.

Edward IV died in 1483 and was quickly succeeded by Edward V, who in turn was succeeded Richard III who reigned untill 1485 when Henry VII assumed power on behalf of the House of Lancaster. Henry built a new four storey, Tudor brick palace replacing all the old buildings except the Great Hall. Fireplaces and chimneys were introduced and offices and houses built for his entourage just outside the palace. Nevertheless Henry preferred to stay at Greenwich in the Palace of Placentia rather than at Eltham. Instead he had his son educated here.

His successor was the celebrated spark of the English Reformation, **Henry VIII.** The new king made further improvements to the palace, installing additional windows, rebuilding the queen's bedroom and moving the chapel to create a larger courtyard. Trees were planted and a pathway ensuring privacy for the troubled monarch ran through a new garden on the south side. Drainage and a sewage system were introduced and a new conduit for bringing in fresh water supplies.

Eltham Palace (photo courtesy of English Heritage, © *Country Life.*)

The palace was a favourite of his queen, **Katharine of Aragon**. Unfortunately, she was divorced by Henry, sparking his battle with the Papacy and the rise of English Protestantism whereby Henry declared himself, and not the Pope, head of the Church of England. Henry then married Anne Boleyn and Eltham ceased to be the main residence of the sovereigns of England. Greenwich became the favourite and Eltham was used as a nursery for the royal children. His successor, Edward VI, never used Eltham and Queen Mary only spent a fortnight there. Queen Elizabeth I stayed for just one night in 1559 and dined there one night in 1576.

The palace was used as a 'grace and favour' house for friends of the royals. Although James I often went hunting in the Eltham grounds he abandoned residence at the palace, preferring to stay in Greenwich while renting out Eltham as apartments to raise cash. One such tenant was the German inventor, **Cornelius Drebble.** He designed a submarine which was rowed under the Thames from London to Greenwich. He also tried to create perpetual motion with his famous contraption, 'the Eltham Motion'.

King Charles II is said to have visited Eltham once, but found it in such a state of disrepair that he never visited again. No other royals would visit the palace for the next 350 years. The parks declined with the fortunes of the palace. Trees were felled in their thousands for shipbuilding at the Woolwich and Deptford timber yards. Deer were slaughtered for food by Cromwell's armies.

John Shaw aquired the palace, now simply the 'Manor of Eltham' at a good price from the king but unable to restore it, he had a new house built in 1664, **Eltham Lodge.** A classic mansion, since 1923 it has been the headquarters of the **Royal Blackheath and Eltham Golf Club**.

Despite some attempts by new owners, the palace fell into further decline. Many of the buildings were stripped of their fittings when Cromwell required timber for his navy. Nor did the locals restrain from availing themselves of the palaces furnishings. Two fireplaces still exist in the **Greyhound Pub** in Eltham. Only the Great Hall and moat bridge remains intact. By 1719 it was being used by farmers as a barn, with the moat later used as a market garden.

ELTHAM

Apart from the Great Hall, the moat and several Tudor buildings, **Eltham Palace** (0208 294 2548 fax 0208 294 2521) includes a tremendous building, **Courtauld House**, with its avante garde interior created for the famous textile manufacturers, the Courtauld family. They bought the palace in 1923 and completed the house in the 1930s to the design of Seely and Paget. In 1944, the Courtaulds surrendered the lease back to the Crown since when it has been used as an army educational establishment.

Stepping out again into the courtyard we admired the first building on the left and closest to the palace. This timber-framed building was the Lord Chancellor's Lodgings when it was built in the 1500s as part of the court coterie's accommodation. Cardinal Wolsey and the great utopian socialist, **Sir Thomas More** would have resided here during the reign of Henry VIII. Heavily restored, it is the only remaining of the 16th century buildings that remains. Nevertheless many of the houses in this row have retained their past names relating to their former palace functions. Chaundrye Close would have been where candles were made, and the Butry, formerly the wine vault.

After leaving the palace, a turn to the right beside the moat takes one into King John's Walk, thought to have been named after the French King, Le Bon. It's a pleasant rustic walk across the fields leading to **Middle Park**. One of the three royal deer parks enclosed in the 1300s, much of the land has been built on. There is a farm which was used as a stud in the mid 19th century by Blenkiron. In 1862 a horse stabled here, Caractacus, won the Derby after the regular jockey had been replaced by a stable lad. Today the Middle Park Stakes remains the biggest race for two-year olds at Newmarket.

Also in the park, the designated **Middle Park Wildlife Area** contains a small lake and is often populated by grazing horses. The Royal Blackheath & Eltham

Golf Course is off Court Rd to the right when leaving the palace. At the southern extremity by Court Road lies **The Tarn**, a delightful area of woodland and gardens surrounding the small lake. The lake, crossed by a wooden bridge, is thought to have been used to stock fish for the palace and 15th century coins have been found on the lake bed. Once part of the grounds, the area still contains the 18th century icewell where ice was cut from the lake and stored. The ice was used to help preserve food and cool drinks served at the Lodge during the warm summer months.

Opposite the Tarn on Middle Park Avenue lies the church of **St Saviours** (tel 0208 850 6829). With its striking purple brick and concrete interior designed by Cachemaille-Day, St Saviours was the first church to be created in a modern style in the London area. It was built for the municipally-owned Middle Park estate in 1933.

Eltham Town Centre

From the palace, Court Road leads north to Well Hall Rd passing through the centre of Eltham to Well Hall. Beside the church and the roadside we saw the old tram shelters erected in the 1920s and now painted yellow and used as public toilets. Opposite St John's Church on the corner, we passed an unusually stylish McDonald's occupying a former, Burton's shop, built during the 1930s. Nearby is a Spanish restaurant which still has the floor mosaics installed when the building was built by Montague Burton in the inter war years.

St John the Baptist Parish

In the centre of Eltham overlooking the main roads through the old village is the church of St John the Baptist. The site has been home to a church since 1115. By 1667 the church had deteriorated to such a poor state that it had to be rebuilt. Work on a new chapel for the new Lord of the Manor, Sir John Shaw, had begun when the roof of the nave collapsed, prompting the rebuilding. The church was again rebuilt in 1875 by Sir Arthur Blomfield and a new spire erected in 1879. The church is particularly noted for its cemetery which includes the sarcophagus of Sir Lady James and her husband of Severndroog Castle fame.

Yemmerrawanyea Kebbara and **Bennelong** were the first native Australians (Aborigines) known to have visited England. They were brought to London by Admiral Arthur Philip in 1792. Kebbara died from tuberculosis or a similar complaint in 1794 at the home of Edward Kent in Eltham. The church yard bears a simple memorial to him. Also buried here (1721) with a memorial is **Thomas Doggett,** founder of what some claim is the world's oldest rowing race, the **Coat and Badge Race.** Opening hours (tel 0208 859 1242) weekdays, 10.30am-1pm, disabled access.

We went off in search of refreshment down Eltham High St. Near to the junction at number 90 is **Mellins Wine Bar and Restaurant** (0208 850 4462, closed Sundays) which began life in 1720 as the village chemist or pharmacy. The owners have an attractive display of old labels used by the apothecarist on the various medicinal and herbal remedies available at the time. With lunch at £3-£5 and a main course at £5-£10 it's an historic place to eat. Mellins also carry 200 or so choices of wine to suit the connoisseur.

Further down at number 183 is the **Electric Café** (0208 859 4095). We sat and drank coffee but could have eaten an Italian style pizza or pasta. It was just too early. Further down on the right we came to Southend Crescent on which stands **Holy Trinity Church**. Built in 1868 it was dedicated to those thousands of soldiers who died in the battles at Gallipoli, during the 1914-18 war. A bell from Sebastopol is on display. Many soldiers from the former Empire countries died during the campaign and the church has been visited by many Commonwealth Prime Ministers.

Left off Eltham High St is Archery Rd where a blue plaque adorns No 55 declaring that it was once home to the Labour leader and Cabinet Minister, **Herbert Morrison**. The area between Archery Rd and Eltham Park to the east is known as the Corbett Estate. **Cameron Corbett** was a former Liberal Member of Parliament for Glasgow. He purchased the land and built the attractive estate. Corbett, a strict Church of Scotland puritan and temperance campaigner, gave all the streets Scottish names and put restrictive clauses in the sale of the houses preventing the sale of alcohol anywhere on the estate.

ELTHAM

A walk further east along Eltham High St led us to Bexley Rd beside which are **Eltham Warren Golf Course**, **Eltham Park South** and, across the railway line, **Eltham Park North**. The area covering the golf course and the south park was known as **The Warren**. It was from springs found here that the palace took its moat's water supply. The flow of water was controlled by a conduit. By Holy Trinity Church one can find the old channel, **Conduit Head,** a 16th century vaulted red brick structure.

Eltham Park South also has a **children's play area**, a **putting green** and **tennis courts**. In the early 19th century **Long Pond** was created as a private lake in Eltham Park North. The pond is now home to ducks and other birds. Part of the park is formed by **Shepherdleas Wood**, part of the ancient forest that covers Shooters Hill. Many of the centuries-old trees were damaged by the great storm which swept south east England in 1987.

Avery Hill

Back on the south side of Bexley Rd we came to Avery Hill, known as the house of 'Colonel' North. This great mansion now sits in the grounds owned by **Greenwich University** in Avery Hill park. The building which today houses the college was built in the 1830's and expanded fourfold by the Colonel after he had bought it in 1882. North bought the surrounding land and diverted the main road to Bexley away from his grounds for his peace and quiet. He spent £200,000 on the interior decoration of the house and had an exquisite winter garden constructed in a glasshouse facing away from the road.

The Italianate style red-brick house designed by TW Cutler had 50 rooms and was noted as an extremely luxurious mansion with marble staircases, picture galleries and sculptures. The stables were panelled in teak and centrally heated. North used the park as a training ground for his horses as he hoped to rival Blenkiron at Middle Park. Pride of place today is the 100 foot square glass roofed winter garden with its many tropical plants and a little home corner of relics rescued from local garden sheds.

The winter garden provides a good view of the park which is now a wide open space. To the right are the old flower beds and rockery, a clue to North's grandiose scheme. Reputed to be quite a character, he is said to have gone to South America to build railways and rumoured to have been involved in gun running in the civil war-ridden continent. But his fortune came from investing in the extraction guano (used to make nitrates) from the continent. A tremendous benefactor for the city of Leeds, he is said to have built Avery Hill to gain acceptance by high society.

North was made an honorary colonel of the Tower Hamlets Yeomanry and seeking a knighthood, invited the Prince of Wales to Avery Hill. **Prince Albert** accepted his invitation but apparently unimpressed, never returned. North never did get his knighthood. However, his eldest son who lived in Lemonwell, secured a knighthood and became Sir Harry North.

To the right of the entry lies a Green Chain walk along a stream which passes a Tudor well head used for diverting water to other well heads. Northwards along Well Hall Rd we turned right into Craigton Road. Number 44 is the former home of film star Bob Hope prior for his departure to Hollywood. His old house carries a blue plaque in commemoration of his stay in Eltham. Local plays and musicals are put on at the **Bob Hope Theatre** (0208 850 3702) on Wythfield Rd. In 1982, before his death, the film star provided assistance to keep the theatre open.

The Manor of Well Hall and the Tudor Barn

We travelled down Well Hall Rd from Eltham centre and soon arrived at the tranquil gardens of Well Hall Manor to our left. The Manor was built around 1400 and owned by the Roper family. As Lord Chancellor, **Thomas More** lived nearby at Eltham Palace and a Roper son, William, married More's daughter Margaret, in 1525.

The Manor was a working farm which the Ropers let to farmers. In 1718 Gregory Page, owner of Wricklemarsh in Blackheath, purchased the Manor, demolished the house and built a new one closer to the road. The rest he continued to lease out. Between the late 19th century and early 20th century the house was lived in by the British novelist and member of the Fabian Society, **Edith Nesbit** and her husband Hubert Bland. On his death she married the captain of the Woolwich Free Ferry and moved away. The house was later demolished.

All that remains of the old Manor is the **Tudor Barn** and the walls around the Pleasance and gardens. The barn may not have been a barn at all but on the front corner one can see **William Roper's** initials. Today the barn serves as a restaurant (tel 0208 768 1774, disabled access). The gardens include a bowling green, a fish pond and a scented garden popular with visitors suffering from impaired vision. The walls of the Pleasance are pocketed with holes known as **Bee Boles** which were used for housing bees.

The Progress Estate

ELTHAM

The Progress Estate lies across Well Hall Rd from **St Barnabas Church**. It was built in just 18 weeks by the authorities to help house the massively expanded Woolwich Arsenal workforce brought in during the 1914-18 war. The estate stands as a monument to the skills of the best craftsmen of the day. Despite having less than five months to erect the houses, they ensured that every house was unique in style. The houses are neither small nor poorly built. Taken over by the Co-operative movement, they are much sought after.

When the Progress estate was built the first church was a hut on Arbroath Rd. In 1916 the estate's worshippers were given an iron church which was finally replaced by the attractive church of St Barnabas in 1933. The church had been the chapel of the **Woolwich Royal Naval Dockyard** since 1858 and was dismantled for its move to Eltham. The building was designed by Sir George Gilbert Scott but the interior was redesigned by Thomas Ford following war damage. It displays a large mural by Hans Feibusch.Opening hours (tel 0208 856 8294) Sunday 8am, service 9.30am. Disabled access.

This part of Eltham is sadly marked by a notorious British murder which occurred during the mid-1990s. A British fascist group had set up their headquarters in Welling. The act led to many clashes between fascists and anti-fascists. The fascists had a small amount of racist support in this area which nevertheless had few ethnic minorities in residence. In 1994, a young black student, **Stephen Lawrence** was murdered by a group of thugs on **Well Hall Rd** close to the bus stop by St Barnabas church.

The police led a desultory investigation. Six years on, the criminals had not been brought to book. Under the weight of protest and condemnation from a legal public inquiry, several senior police officers retired or left the force. For the first time the British establishment formally accepted that institutionalised racism exists – at least that is, in the police force.

CHARLTON **The Village**

The centre of Charlton, although sometimes called Charlton should correctly be called The Village. Mentioned in the Domesday Book of 1086 as Cerletone, it was recorded as one of a score of 'free villages' in England. Hence while Greenwich gave allegiance to the Abbey of Ghent, The Village gave allegiance only to the king. The word, 'Charlie' was used to describe a free person. Today, Charlton can claim to be the only true 'village' in London

Arriving at **Charlton House**, it's easy to recognise the basic aspects of the old village. The manor was pulled down to make way for Charlton House which, with the church and the public house beside it look onto the village green. The road passing by was the main road to Greenwich. Following the narrow path it has followed for centuries, though a main road today, it still twists and turns its way through the village. Charlton, midway between Eltham Palace and Greenwich Palace became an important stop off point. Many a royal would drop into Charlton House, mention of which can be found in the famous diaries of Samuel Pepys and John Evelyn. Today its rooms are more popular with film directors than royalty.

Charlton House

Charlton House stands at the centre of the village, and is said to be one of the finest examples of Jacobean domestic architecture in Britain. Before the house is a large green at the centre of which are columns supporting an arched, neo-classical mock gate. Seeing it up close, it's obvious that it would have been too narrow for a coach and horses to pass through. Besides, none of the old plans show a path through the arch. Entry would have been by the two side gates. The arch marked the original perimeter of the house grounds but the owners gradually encroached to take over the green.

To the right of the gate is the mansion's garden summer house designed by **Inigo Jones** and once used by the council authorities as a public toilet – one of the most fashionable in the country.

Beside the garden house is a beautiful mulberry tree. It is said to have been planted by **King James I**. The king was interested in developing the silk industry in Britain and many houses connected with the Stuart king have a mulberry tree within their grounds. However, this was the black mulberry (instead of the white mulberry) and did not bear silkworms. It does, however, bear fruit which is harvested for jam to raise money if the berries can be pickedbefore the kids have snaffled them.

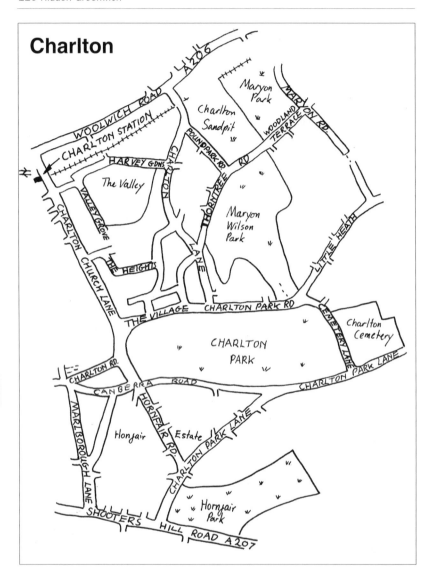

Charlton

CHARLTON

To the left of the house is the old stable block, now used as council offices. And at the centre is a large green over which looks the magnificent mansion facade of red brick relieved with white quoins and dressings. Shaped like a shallow H with slight protruding cross pieces at each end, the facade also has a wonderfully decorous porch with heraldic symbols. The house with its Flemish

Charlton House

design is thought to be the work of ***John Thorpe***, an associate of Inigo Jones.

We entered the large hall. Above the east door hung the coat of arms of the Prince of Wales. The coat reveals the story for Charlton House was built between 1607 and 1612 to be the tutorial quarters of Prince Henry, eldest son of James I, and the home of Adam Newton, his tutor. Newton was Dean of Durham and part of the royal staff till 1629. However, Prince Henry died before the house could be completed. When Newton died in 1629 the house passed to his son who, being a royalist, had to leave his family in the house while he left to take part in the Civil War.

Inigo Jones, Renaissance Designer, Architect and Painter

Originally a painter and a draughtsman, Inigo Jones took up the ideas and spirit of the Renaissance and put them to work in his architecture. He became Britain's most famous Renaissance designer and was responsible for architecting many royal palaces and gardens. A man of many talents, Jones was also an author of a book on Stonehenge, a theorist and an antiquarian. Not content with creating the royal palaces, at the Stuart court he would design the scenery and costumes for the royal masquerades and balls.

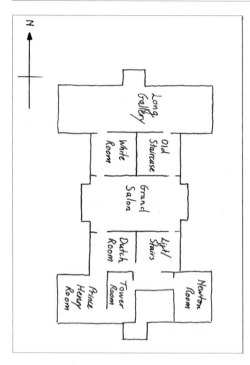

The house and position of Lord of The Manor then passed through several hands including those of the royally connected Maryon Jones family until 1777. One of them was a William Langhorne who had been British Governor of Madras. At 84 he married a 17 year old girl but died hierless though happy.

Ghost hunters arrive from miles around to spend nights in the house said to be haunted by his ghost. Some time ago two of the managers at the centre felt a powerful and frightening feeling. Since then the story has grown up around the bawdy ghost. Ghost hunters say that they have heard strange noises on the stairs and apparitions have been seen near the secret entrance to Mary Langhorne's office. It is also said that sometimes a ghost chases ladies around and one can feel the ladies' presence.

Eventually, the property was inherited by the wife of Sir Thomas Spencer Wilson. Her daughter, Jane Wilson eloped and married **Spencer Perceval** who, depite being disapproved of by the family, lived in the house for some time. However, once elected as Prime Minister, his status improved. Never-theless he has the distinction of being the first Prime Minister of Britain to be assassinated – and in the House of Commons at that.

After Jane Wilson's death the house went to her son, Sir Thomas Maryon-Wilson. The Maryon-Wilson's owned much of Charlton and Woolwich and counted Princess Charlotte among their friends. The estate and house remained in the family for the next century. Having many children, the Maryon-Wilsons expanded the house and the south wing was extended in 1870, providing for a games room and bedrooms to the design of Norman Shaw.

In the **1914-1918 War** the house was part used as a military hospital, with officers tended to in the house, while ordinary troops were accommodated under canvas marquees in the grounds. The Maryon-Wilson tenure finally ended when Sir Spencer Maryon-Wilson sold the estate to the council in 1925. Today the mansion is a community centre, surely one of the most historic in the land.

Despite its current use the authorities have taken care to preserve the originality of the decorations and design of the Grade 1 listed building. Standing in the hall, as we looked up from the coffee bar we could see the attractive flat strap work that adorns the ceiling. The hall rises for two storeys, the lower part of the walls being panelled and the upper retaining the hooks once used to drape tapestries. The height of the ceiling allowed for a gallery or balcony on the first floor. It was introduced above the entrance by the third owner, Ducie, and links the two wings of the house.

The doorway to the Wilson Room (once the dining room) and the doorway to the Chapel are decorated with twelve panels at the top of which are the boar's head crest of Newton and the stag crest of the Puckerings, his wife's family. To the left a beautiful oak staircase with its heavily moulded handrail and balustrade rose to the first floor. It becomes even more ornate as one ascends to the second floor. The bottom section contains Doric strapwork, the middle, Ionian and the top, Corinthian.

Directly above the hall, designed to the same shape and size is the Grand Salon. We entered noting the huge heavy doors with their monstrous bolts and hinges.

Looking up we gazed at the richly decorated ceiling with its hanging pendants, the largest of which is in the middle. The marble and alabaster fireplace watched over by Vulcan and Venus was the work of **Nicholas Stone**, stonemason to James I. We turned to the west bay and then to the east, taking note of the royal insignia. The west carries the Stuart coat of arms and the initials of James I, while the east bay has the Prince of Wales feathers, the Garter and the motto, '*Ich Dien*'.

The panelled Dutch Room, once a bedroom, is linked to the Grand Salon. We entered to admire its chimney breast in black marble, and a frieze decorated with fruit, jewels and various flora. The White Room, probably used as a small function room, adjoins the Grand Salon and is opposite the Dutch Room. It has a marvellous fireplace above which is a frieze illustrating the Triumph of Christ and the Triumph of Death and piety, mercy and peace. The overmantel has an oval panel at its heart depicting Pegasus and Perseus holding the head of Medusa.

We doubled back through the White Room and into the impressive Long Gallery. 70ft in length, the passage is illuminated by light streaming through stain glass windows bearing Ducie's coat of arms. The carefully restored strap work on the ceiling has three lozenge shaped panels. The frieze, looking down on a marble fireplace, is decorated with dogs, masks matching the frieze and flora. Its also a popular place for Wild Bill's ghost to float above the wooden floor.

Lady Newton's bedroom is worth a look for its fireplace with its erotic depictions of Perseus and two women, half mermaid and half horse. Descending, we went into what is currently a bar area. Once the library, it has a solid oak fireplace installed in 1612. The wing currently housing the public lending library served as the chapel and a small dining room. We went outside to view the rear of the house which looked onto large grounds. The two dozen and more mock Tudor chimneys on the roof are quite a sight if you can get a guide to take you up there.

The gardens today cover a very small part of the former grounds which stretched to Woolwich Common. They included what is now Charlton Park and the Cemetery. Traces of the former kitchen and floral gardens remain and we could only imagine how the gardens would have appeared, adorned with its many statues which existed here. The rear and front of the house have plenty of ancient plane trees – said to be excellent counters in the past to London's once heavily polluted atmosphere.

Charlton House (tel 0208 856 3591)is **open** all year round and available for weddings, meetings and other functions. There is a lift to all floors but **disability access** remains limited because of the labyrinth of corridors and steps. **Guided tours** are available. As we left a couple were making arrangements to be married just before the beginning of the London Marathon and so be able to take part in the famous 26-mile race.

From the rear of the house one can look over to **Charlton Park**. The park's tall 17th century brick walls testify that it was once part of the mansion's grounds. Today it is a large open space with a **children's play area.**

CHARLTON

Charlton Church Lane

Leaving the house and turning left into Charlton Church Lane, we came across the church of **St Lukes**, which was part of the green. A previous church existed on the site but the current brick church was erected in 1630 at the behest of Sir Adam Newton who had bequeathed the money. Some years ago while treating the building for dry rot, workmen fell through the floor onto coffins in the crypt. It's not sure whether the workmen returned but their shock was history's gain as local historians were able to view remnants of the old church.

Sir Adam and his wife, Lady Katherine left money for the building of the church, their generosity commemorated with a large black and white marble monument sculpted by Nicholas Stone who worked both for royalty and Charlton House. Also buried here is William Langhorne. The church was maintained with support from the owners of the manor.

Many officers of the Woolwich Artillery are buried at the church which also has a monument to **Spencer Perceval**, the only British Prime Minister to have been assassinated to date. He was buried in the church grounds in 1812.

Sarcophagi vie with the large gravestones for prominence. Another tomb is that of Edward Wilkinson (1574), Yeoman of the Vale and Master Chef to Henry VIII, Elizabeth and Edward VI. **Opening hours** (tel 0208 858 8175) Tues and Thurs, 10.00am-2pm, Sunday 10am. **Disabled access.**

The trough and memorial fountain immediately in front of the church were introduced in 1902 to commemorate the coronation of Edward VII. In the 1980s a car crashed into the drinking fountain, completely demolished it. The village mounted a successful fund-raising campaign to restore it to its former glory. The cage and stocks for punishing petty criminals stood on the green but have since been moved to a spot near the trough.

The main road boasts several picturesque cottages. A section of one of the two pubs dates back to the 1700s, with the former bakery being built during the late 1600s. There are two tandoori curry houses in the village, which would have been officers' houses in the 1800s. Elaborate Victorian iron work adorns the facades.

Further on to the left are the **Assembly Rooms** with a Dutch gable built in the 1800s to celebrate the marriage of the eldest son of the Maryon-Wilsons and later given to the people. Next door is an arch, the former gate to the army drill hall built in the 1870s.

On Fairfield Grove we came to the first council houses built in the Greenwich area. Erected in 1919, they had the attention of the Guild of Master Builders of the area. What the people gained in housing they lost in recreation for the grounds on which the houses stood were the traditional grounds of the **Horn Fair** which centred on Charlton House.

Held every October 18th, the Horn Fair had been a popular annual event protected by Charter since the 14th century. Folklore has it that **King John** visited Charlton and made a miller's daughter pregnant. In deference to the miller, King John handed him a large area of land and the fair became the village's annual celebration. Indeed around Charlton there was once a saying, 'All's fair at Horn Fair'

October 18th is **St Luke's Day**. With St Luke's being the local church and St Luke's emblem being a horned beast, it is suggested by historians that the Horn Fairtook its name from the church.

At the fair most men would wear horns on their heads and every stall would display horns. Many men dressed as women while others carried sprigs of furze with which to tickle the women. The fair became a bawdy event and in 1872 it became too riotous for the owners and it was moved away from the house. The fair was resurrected at the house 25 years ago by the people of Charlton and it continues as the main fair in the area, but without the usual drunkenness and debauchery of its earlier years.

Close to Fairfield Grove are St Lukes Almshouses for the poor. Such buildings have existed on the site since the 1690s but these were rebuilt in 1706 with money left by William Langhorne to build a school on the top floor. Painted in lemon, the properties have wonderful twisting oak props installed in 1839 supporting the arcade.

The two cemeteries, which were once on Maryon-Wilson land, are on Cemetery Lane and contain several interesting tombs and sarcophagi. There are two chapels, one being for Church of England mourners, and the other for other denominations.

We went onto **Charlton Athletic Football Club** close to Horn Lane. Charlton is the closest main line station to the Dome and is due to run a coach transfer service to the attraction. The station is located on Charlton Church Lane, opposite is Wing Ching's Vietnamese restaurant. To the right is a main post office and further up the hill the **Valley Cafe** serving inexpensive food at £2 to £5 from 6.30am till 4.30pm. Across from the cafe is the road which led us down to the Soccer stadium.

Charlton Athletic Football Club, founded in 1905, has a history in the Football League dating back to 1921. Anyone remotely interested in soccer and the community will find a trip to their ground at **The Valley** on Floyd Road enlightening. The club's story is not simply one of players and managers but one of a community fighting for its right to watch top class football.

The Valley also holds many records. The massive ground once held 75,000 spectators, a figure unrivalled by most of the capital's other clubs. The East Stand claimed to be the world's biggest football terrace. The club was also the first to televise live soccer matches. In the post war years The Valley was the biggest club stadium in the country.

CHARLTON

In 1974 the Valley entered the Guinness Book of records as the venue for a concert of famous rock band, The Who, and another international star, Lou Reed. The band staged the noisiest outdoor concert ever recorded at that time.

In its early days the ground had to be dug out of the sand and in 1919 volunteer supporters were called in to carry out the excavations. Their work paid off and Charlton ascended to the top flight First Division of the Football League. From 1937, the club remained at this level for 21 years. In this time they made several appearances at Wembley including two in the FA Cup Final. In 1947, with the assistance of goalkeeper and football immortal Sam Bartram, Charlton won the FA Cup.

The Battle to Save The Valley and Charlton Athletic

After 1958, the club suffered a chequered history, plummeting to the lowest divisions of the Football League. By the 1980s Charlton would break another record.

They were the first club to be served with a winding up notice by a fellow League member. The club was in a financial mess and had not paid Leeds United an agreed transfer fee for their winger, Carl Harris.

The writing seemed to be on the wall and a Save Charlton Action Committee was set up, collecting donations in buckets to pay part of the transfer fee for new player, Ronnie Moore. With the club being ordered to be wound up by the courts, club Chairman, Mr Hulyer, made his final offer of £30,000 from a Swiss bank account and other money dependent on the progress of a shipment of rubber, in order to keep hold of his asset.

The official receiver ordered the gates locked and Charlton had to postpone one match before a solution could be found. New player Ronnie Moore was kicked out of his lodgings in Blackheath's Clarendon Hotel for fear that the club could not pay his bill. At this point Greenwich Borough Council promised to inject £250,000 as part of a new bid to save the club. The bid was successful and television pundit, Jimmy Hill, became temporary Chairman for six months.

Having been reprieved, the club then faced a new threat. Part of the ground was unsafe and rather than invest in restoring it, the directors moved the club out of The Valley to Selhurst Park in Croydon. Apart from being the cherished home of rival Crystal Palace, the ground was also a long road journey through heavily congested streets. Disgruntled Charlton supporters staged pitch invasions in protest but in vain.

The club were actually successful on the pitch while at Selhurst Park and once again reached the then top flight First Division of the League. However, fans were boycotting the trip to Selhurst Park and, despite reaching Wembley again in 1987, with the likes of footballer, now turned television presenter, Garth Crooks, and Carl Leaburn, some of the match attendance figures were the lowest in the club's history.

In 1988 a supporter's fanzine, Voice of The Valley, was set up independent of the club directors and campaigning for the club's return to Charlton. A battle raged in the press and in the town halls. Thousands backed the campaign and several town hall meetings saw 1,000 people turn up.

By 1989 the directors were behind the scheme. The Valley ground had suffered from years of neglect. It had been hit by the 1987 hurricane and arsonists, and became a site for itinerant travellers. With litter, debris and weeds covering the ground, ferns grew as high as a man on the terraces. The club expected the clean-up to take several weeks. They appealed for help from the supporters. Hundreds turned up and the ground was cleared within one day.

Within the council opposition began to stir based on the inconvenience for Charlton residents having the club on its doorstep. A new battle was on. Consultation meetings were even held in Charlton House. Voice of the Valley then engaged in a new campaign and, with the supporters' club, set up the Valley Party to contest the council elections in Greenwich Borough. 60 candidates stood contesting 62 seats. Hundreds turned out in support. The poster campaign was so successful and innovative that it won several advertising industry awards. The Valley Party took more than 14,000 (12%) of the total vote. Many candidates came in ahead of those of the established parties and one keen opponent of the campaign to return to The Valley was removed from the council.

The battle wasn't over but support stayed strong. In 1991 2,000 fans turned up to a council meeting held at Woolwich Town Hall. Victory was eventually won but peace was still a while away. The club left Croydon but The Valley was not ready for the start of the 1991/2 season and for 15 months used West Ham in the East End as their home ground.

After the traumatic decade, it is easy to imagine the delight in Charlton when in 1998 the team went to Wembley and won the play off final taking them into the Premier League. Charlton would see top flight football for the first time in 41 years. For the people of Charlton the victory was the perfect conclusion to a story of decline and revival in which many of them played a part.

When news of the club's promotion to the Premier League reached Charlton, the whole area came alive with horns and sirens sounding all night long. The team were given the freedom of the borough. Conquering heroes from Wembley Stadium, they returned to the village on an open top bus followed by thousands of supporters.

Club director and lifelong fan, Michael Grade, head of Channel 4 Television paid tribute: "The fans have played a critical role over the last seven years to bring about probably the most remarkable transition ever seen in the football world. If you had told me in the early nineties that in 1998 we would be playing in the Premiership and in one of the most modern stadiums in the country, I'd have said that you were barking mad."

We visited the club just after they had just slipped back into the First Division. We entered the plush new offices in the main stand. At the reception stood two cups, one of which was a replica of the cup won by the club when they won the 1998 play-off final. The stand has four floors with **disability access** to the main suites which are now not only used for matches but hired out for functions such as weddings, parties, dinners and conferences. They also include a modern gym and sports' injury treatment centre and the **Floyd's** sports bar which is able to cater for up to 200 people. All these facilities are open to the public. Along the corridors hang pictures commemorating the club's 95 proud years.

Today the all-seater stadium has a capacity of 20,000 spectators. It is very attractive with trees providing a green edging to three surrounds. The club has several suites available for hire and boast the best conference facilities in South East London. The **Millennium Suite** holds 700 people, the Meridian 150, the Greenwich 60 and the clubs boardroom with its own bar, 18. They are all topped by the **Observatory Suite** holding 150 with its magnificent views of the Dome, Thames Barrier, National Maritime Museum and the Cutty Sark.

Reflecting its past history, Charlton Athletic have retained a strong link with the community and work closely with Greenwich Borough Council. It has a special room equipped with **computers for children** to do their homework while being visited by their favourite footballers. It has a strong **anti-racist** profile and is committed to action against racism, both in the ground and in the local community. Matches are played between mid-August and May, usually on alternate Saturdays and occasionally mid-week (tel 0208 333 4000). The club's website can be found at **www.cafc.co.uk**

Tours (tel 0208 333 4010) guided by Charlton veterans are available for visitors to the ground. Disability access is good and there is a special viewing areas reserved for match days.

Towards the Thames

Left out of the train station at the bottom of Charlton Church Lane on the corner of Woolwich Rd we found a McDonald's opposite The **Waterman pub**. Continuing on down Anchor & Hope Lane we found the **Anchor & Hope pub** beside the jetty on the riverside.

Moving inland we passed through beautiful woodland on Sauntering Road in **Hanging Wood**. Some say the woods took their name from the lynching of highwaymen.

The Newgate Calendar tells the tale of two brigands who, run down by the whole of the Woolwich garrison, "imitated the example of hunted foxes and had gone to earth in an old drain." The men were discovered down the drain and put on trial. Despite the tale, it's more likely that the name refers to the hanging trees.

Hanging Wood is part of **Maryon-Wilson Park**, so called because the land was donated to the municipality in 1912. We visited the park on Thorntree Road. It contains an **animal farm** enclosure and a **deer park**. With its trees and the mounds, split by several streams and accompanied by **rare plant** species, it is rather eye-catching for such a small stretch of land and a good place to take children. However, don't confuse it with Maryon Park. This small, more formal park is on the Woolwich Road and frequented by foxes. It features **Cox's Mount** so-called because the park was rented in 1838 by a Mr Cox who planted poplars in the park.

CHARLTON

Excavations show that the site was once a hill fort of a Romano-British clan which flourished during the Romans' 400 year occupation of Britain. In the 1850s the mount was used to adjust ships' compasses. The area was used for sand works which created many of the dips and hollows.

Close by on Charlton Lane is **Gilberts Pit**, an immense sand pit dug during Georgian times when sand adorned London's parlour floors instead of carpets. The exposed strata of rock have made the pit a geologist's haunt and special paths have been arranged for visitors to see this protected site.

Back on East Moor Street beside the Thames, Charlton is also home to the **Thames Barrier** (tel 0208 845 1373). The biggest movable flood barrier in the world, it took 8 years to build. The Thames Barrier Visitors' Centre can also be reached by taking the ferry from **Greenwich Pier**.

Moored close by is a **Russian submarine** which saw service in the Soviet fleet between 1967 and 1994. A reminder of the Cold War between the West and the East, its engine rooms and cramped crew's quarters are open to the public. **Opening hours** (tel 0208 855 7560) are in summer daily between 10am and 6pm and in winter, from 10am till dusk.

WOOLWICH **and its Imperial Past**

Woolwich was once home to the Arsenal (including the football team), six army barracks and a naval dockyard. By 1903, nine out of ten of the Woolwich workforce, were employed by the government. Nowadays most of the troops have gone but evidence of the military presence and the troops used to build Britain the largest empire the world has ever known, is all over the district. The town is still the home of the **Royal Artillery**, while fine buildings, parade grounds, old jetties and gates, foundries and cannons, are scattered along the river bank.

However, Woolwich had its own history before the army took to its streets. In 1853 workers digging at the Arsenal discovered Roman burial urns, and subsequently a **Roman burial ground** was found beneath what is now Dial Square. The settlement is believed to have stood at the site of the old power station.

There is also evidence of a later Saxon church which once stood on a sand hill lapped by the Thames. Eventually the Thames won, washing away the sand, resulting in the collapse of the church. A new church was built further inland and the 11th century Domesday Book records that a settlement existed here known as Hulviz. Unlike other parts of the borough, Woolwich, a small riverside town built on sand mounds, was never a manor in the Middle Ages. It was originally part of Eltham and its workers supplied Eltham Palace. The parish covered no more than 3.5 miles compared to Charlton's 11 miles. Most of what is now Woolwich Common was then Charlton Common.

In 1512, **Henry VIII** established his **Royal Dockyard** here for the building of his royal flagship, the Great Harry. Woolwich dockyards remained in use until 1869, when its final closure precipitated mass unemployment.

Coming down from Shooters Hill besides the old police station, we turned right and eastwards along Academy Road, finding the **Royal Military Academy** on the left, easily identified by the 15 or so big cannons and guns lined up outside facing the road. Until 1945, the Academy was the training ground for the Royal Artillery's cadets and the sister academy to Sandhurst, now Britain's premier officer training school. Between 1741 and 1808, the Academy was based at the Arsenal before moving to this building.

The building has a 720ft long facade designed in yellow brick with stone dressing by Wyatt in 1806. The central block design was based on the White Tower in the Tower of London in a Gothic style. The lead topped bell tower with its weathervane has huge sloping slats which allowed the now silenced bells to ring out around the common. Sadly it has fallen into disrepair and the base is hardly used. Nevertheless it remains intact enough and is popular with film

WOOLWICH

Military Woolwich

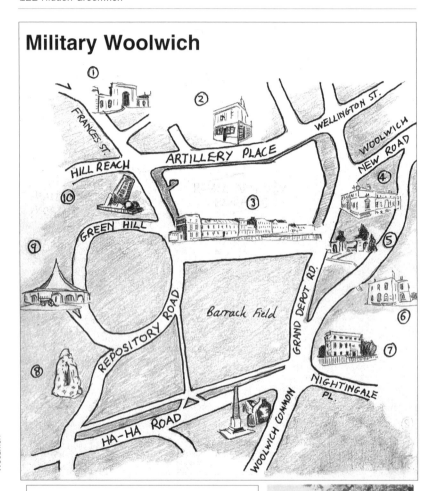

Key

1. Cambridge Barracks House
2. Army House Pub
3. Royal Artillery B arracks
4. Connaught Mews
5. Royal Garrison Church of St George
6. Engineer House
7. Government House
8. Afghan/Zulu war memorial
9. Rotunda Museum
10. Mallet's Mortar

production companies and the TV series, Bramwell, had filmed there. The top floor houses the **Royal Artillery History Museum** which has an excellent collection of banners, standards and uniforms, as well as items celebrating the Royal Artillery's history since its creation in 1716. The museum is closed and will re-open at the Arsenal in 2001 (tel 0208 781 5628).

After requesting that the police at the Red Lion Lane police sentry post contact the verger, we entered the **Royal Garrison Church of St. Michael & All Angels**. Invited in we took the long walk along Middle Road through the centre of the base taking, advantage of the good view of the Barracks interior. The barracks has a fine collection of early 19th century battlemented red brick buildings with small turrets, a few of which are used as offices for the military police and Ministry of Defence administrators. The other buildings remain empty.

The Royal Garrison church was begun in 1902, as the Royal Garrison Church on Grand Depot Rd was too far away to attract cadets in sufficient numbers. From 1863 they attended the Garrison Church of St George but it was a mile away and by 1886 the matter had even reached the pages of The Times newspaper.

The new Garrison church's foundation stone was finally laid in 1903. Designer, Major Hemming R.E, gave the church a rather military appearance with its copper covered turret and battlements. The building was made from red brick with Doulton stone dressing to match the Academy buildings. The oak roof was covered with green Westmoreland slates and the flooring designed in a simple pattern of red Mansfield and Portland stone. Measuring 86ft by 30ft, it would seat 300 cadets and soldiers.

Originally, the base was known as The Shop where cadets would train for up to two years to get up to standard. The church was built for £8,000. At this time the chapel was simply brick work. When the base at Addiscombe was closed parts of their chapel, including the wooden choirs, were transferred to the Academy. Consequently, the decorations include items from the East India Company and the Royal Ordnance Corps. The stained glass window with St George, St Andrew and St David flanking Christ in the apse comes from the surviving cadets of the Royal East India Company. In the rerodos Christ blesses Doubting Thomas.

The church had no organ and the current organ was introduced much later. Where it stands today was once a gallery for the soldier staff of the base. The main church had been located on Grand Depot Road which was bombed in the war. The verger commented, "It was much bigger than this church. I used to go there with my father on a Sunday just to watch the Sunday parade. They'd come out with their band in front and march down the road. It was quite something."

An old Toc H lamp is on display, one of the five Toc H lamps used on the front line during the 1914-1918 war, and presented to the church by Edward, Prince of Wales in 1926. The church was also intended as a campo santo for memorials to graduates from the Academy who died in service and the walls are covered with brass or copper plate commemorations to the cadets who never survived. Regimental pendants and others commemorating battles hang on the wall.

"Some of these cadets were lucky to see three or four weeks after they left the Academy," said the Verger. "They left here at 18 and you can see from the memorial plaques on the walls that many died within two or three years. An officer's standard life in the 1914-18 war was about a fortnight. Half of them died at 18 or 20 years old. A church at the top of Shooters Hill records the thousands of soldiers who passed that way and never came back."

Kitchener was at the Academy and is commemorated in the nave, which has a hammerbeam oak roof, giving the appearance of an upturned ship's keel. The only momento of the 1939-1945 war is a reef to Royal Artillery officers killed in action at the Battle of Kohima against Japan.

The magnificent stained glass window opposite the apse was created by Christopher Whall in 1920. If you stand back and look carefully you can see that the window portrays the very first artillery band in uniform and gunners with their cannons who fought during the Napoleonic, Crimean and 1914-1918 wars. Badges of the Royal Engineers and the Royal Artillery, General Bogard, as well as French and Belgian soldiers are included. The Archangel Gabriel and St Michael are accompanied by cherubs.

By prior arrangement, the friendly verger will arrange for visitors to see the other books and military memorabilia collected by the Garrison church. The record book of the Academy details life in the Barracks, the changing uniforms and armaments between 1741 and 1892

Outside and opposite the church we visited a small, pretty courtyard, pond and fountain, over which looked the new arrivals' office of the Academy. This building, together with the vast officers mess', library, and bar had more of an appearance of an Oxford college than the muddy horror which would meet these young officers when they left for 'man's little hour'. We walked back through the base to the imaginary sounds of the cadets on drill, the whinnying of the horses and the rattles of the carts.

WOOLWICH

The church, still available for weddings etc, can be seen by appointment with the verger John Hookins (tel 0208 781 5627) who is available on Mondays, Wednesdays and Fridays or by attending the Sunday service at 11am.

Heading east again, we passed **Woolwich Common** where the artillery used to practise lobbing shells, which would often fly over the roads and sometimes onto Shooters Hill. The Common, which extended to Charlton, was encroached upon by the army and a great deal of land was taken over by the Royal Artillery in 1774. In 1802 the Common was bought by the Ordnance Board for use as a drill ground. While one can freely amble across its pastures, it is still controlled today by the Ministry of Defence. However, as if to underline their ownership,

The Rotunda

the Defence Ministry still announce it's closure on one day of each year.

To the right we also passed a set of flats built on the site where **General Gordon of Khartoum** (who trained at the Royal Military Academy) was born. We then turned left beside an old stone horses' trough and strolled into Haha Rd, so called not because it's a funny place to live, but because a ditch built there resembling an Indian ha ha ditch. The ditch was used to keep grazing cattle away from the Royal Artillery's parade ground.

We passed through the former army sentry post onto Repository Road which led us to the army's **Royal Military Repository**, established in 1805 as a training and storage area. To the left was a pile of roughly hewn stones mounted with copper trophies, a memorial to the British forces who fought during the Afghan War and the Zulu Wars in South Africa. The Zulu wars were brought back to popular awareness by the films, Zulu Dawn and Zulu featuring Michael Caine and other well known film stars.

The trucks of the Royal Artillery sat parked behind the wire paled in significance compared to the 25ft cannon mounted on a transporter positioned beside them. Suddenly I realised that this was no museum. This was an example of the hardware used by the British Army. Eventually we did come to three old cannons at the gates of the **Artillery's Rotunda Museum** which is due to move to Woolwich Arsenal. Off the main road and little known, this museum is a must for those interested in military history and even carries contemporary history.

Sited close to the entrance is a huge pipe, part of the notorious British-made Iraqi Supergun which never reached Saddam Hussain's army. The display also includes a couple of Russian-made Iraqi guns captured during the Gulf War.

Some machines appear like tanks but they are actually self-propelled guns which fire from a stationery position up to 20 miles from the target. Tanks are able to fire on the move. Other guns such as the 105 mm light gun are still in service.

The collection has been assembled since 1778 as part of artillery training. It includes not only 600 years of British guns but enemy munitions captured as trophies, and others such as the two Chinese Ming dynasty guns. A wrought-iron cannon mounted in wood from Henry VIII's warship the **Mary Rose**, and a dragon gun from the Mandalay palace of the king of Burma, are also on display.

The prize of the museum is its principal building, the Rotunda, a tent taken from Hyde Park, once used by the kings and dukes of the countries who prematurely celebrated victory over Napoleon at Waterloo in 1814. In this Regency masterpiece, the allies re-divided the world and the spoils of victory. The tent was originally erected in the grounds of the Prince Regent and housed many a royal party celebrating the defeat of Napoleon

John Nash was a Georgian architect of the picturesque movement. Later, Nash had the idea of enveloping the tent in a polygonal outer shell of yellow brick, and covering the canvas roof with tiles. It still stands today. The museum will eventually move to The Arsenal. One bonus is it affords beautiful views of the top of Shooters Hill. Opening Hours, weekdays, 1pm-4pm. (tel 0208 781 3127)

The Parade Ground and the Royal Artillery Barracks

WOOLWICH

We couldn't get into the Royal Artillery Barracks on Repository Rd but the gates offer a tremendous view of the magnificent 1,000ft long façade, said to be the longest Georgian facade in Britain. The gleaming white building displays a triumphal arch at its centre, flanked by a tripartite range of buildings. The eastern half was built between 1775 and 1782 while the west was added to the design of James Wyatt in 1802.

Today, the facade is all that is left of the original barracks, the rear having been modernised to hold the 16th Artillery regiment. The left side housed the mess and The Silver Room which includes trophies such as a palm tree candelabrum presented by William IV, a golden ram's head from Africa and the Empress Eugenie Shield presented by Eugenie, Napoleon II's wife in 1858.

The Parade Ground used for passing out parades almost on the scale of Trooping the Colours, lies before the barracks and stretches even further. It was originally paved with red gravel brought from Shooters Hill. Nearby stands the Crimea War memorial erected in 1860. The bronze statue of Victory was designed by John Bell. Close to that is the Dixon Memorial to General Sir

Alexander Dixon and his son. The General was a master gunner and the two guns beside the memorial are those from which all Victoria Cross medals are cast. The splendid captured 17th century **Bhurtpore Gun** is decorated with lions and tigers and was cast for the Mogul Ruler of India, Emperor Aurangzeb in 1677. After 150 years of use by the Moguls it was captured at the siege of Bhurtpore in 1827 and handed over to the Royal Artillery as a trophy by George IV in 1828.

A red 1927 K2 telephone box stands abandoned at the end of the Parade ground. At the opposite end and across Grand Depot Road lies the Royal Garrison Church of St George. Not to be confused with the Garrison Church of St Michael at the Royal Academy, the church was designed by Thomas Henry Wyatt in 1863 in the Byzantine/Italianate style he had used in the church at Wilton. Stock bricks with red and blue vitrified brick trimmings were used and the interior contained marble works and mosaics.

The church was bombed during the last war and the interior is rather weather beaten. Today the site is maintained as part of a memorial garden occasionally used for open air church services. Visits by appointment (tel 0208 781 3712)

Just north of the church on Grand Depot Rd is Connaught Mews. Built in 1780 to house the **Royal Ordnance Hospital** it was enlarged in 1806 and became known as Connaught Barracks in 1865. South of the church across Woolwich New Rd lies Engineer House which was built in 1803 as part of the Royal Engineer Barracks. Today it is used as a community centre for the military and their families. Woolwich New Rd was once chillingly known as Cholic Lane, the main road through to London. South of Engineer House is Government House with its facade of brown stock brick and stone string courses. It was built in the early 1800s and has a high brick parapet above the projecting porch.

Leaving the Parade ground and slightly further down Repository Road opposite the Barracks to our left we saw **Mallet's Mortar** on display in the grounds. The mortar was designed in 1854 by Robert Mallet to lob shells during the Crimean War. Tested in 1858 it lobbed a 2,359lb shell for around 3,000 metres (2,759 yards). The mortar was never used.

Continuing down Repository Road we crossed a junction into Frances St where, to our right, stood Cambridge Barracks Gatehouse, erected to guard the Cambridge Barracks built in 1847 to house Royal Marines. Today the Gatehouse stands alone, the barracks having long since been replaced by council housing.

The Royal Arsenal

Further down river and past the ferry station on Warren Lane, we came to Royal Arsenal West. Once known as Woolwich Warren because of the farming of rabbits in the area, the site was initially used by the military during the 1500s as a location for military stores. In 1667, with the threat of Dutch attacks, Prince Rupert was ordered to fortify the site. A 16th century mansion, Tower

Place, was bought at the west end of 'The Warren' and used to accommodate the Lieutenant General of Ordnance. In 1695 the Royal Laboratory moved to the Warren to make fireworks and gunpowder.

The Ordnance factory was founded in 1720 to make weapons. Prior to its establishment military hardware was produced in the area, as evidenced by Ordnance Wharf which had already been in existence for some time. An explosion at Moorfields in 1718 had alerted the authorities to the dangers of casting big guns in populated areas and ordnance work was moved to the banks of the Thames, establishing the first Crown gun foundry.

The cadets moved in later and became recruits for the Royal Military Academy with the Artillery Academy moving to its present location in 1806. By this time, 10,000 people were employed at the Warren within walls built by convict labour that extended initially for 2.5 miles before being extended to 5 miles. Many a ship's hulk was used for the walls which still stand today. The rabbits may have left the Warren but the plentiful food stores and left-overs attracted hundreds of wild cats. Although cat catchers were employed, many soldiers would free cats from their traps and feed them.

During the 1914-1918 war a colossal 80,000 workers were employed at the Arsenal. Many were women and the experience gave many women who lived in the area a new confidence in their own industrial muscle. Soon after, women won the right to vote. The Arsenal itself went into decline, manufacturing shells but little else.

Apart from a few storemen, excavators, restorers and military police, the Arsenal is now deserted. Some of its buildings will be demolished, leaving 23 listed buildings reflecting British imperial, military and architectural heritage. When we arrived some were being used to store material for the National Maritime Museum.

Looking through the gates to our right we saw the oldest of the buildings, the Royal Laboratory Pavilions begun in 1695 and carrying the date 1698 with the arms of King William III. Built in brick with stone quoins, shapely doorways and window surrounds, each pavilion had five bays. Behind lay the **Royal Brass Foundry** built in 1717, once attributed to **Sir John Vanbrugh**, and now preserved as a listed building. The red brick building has stone dressing and was restored in 1970. The projecting piers with stripes of Portland stone and rubbed brick on each side of the entrance with the royal arms above, makes it an impressive sight. The interior has not been restored to its original design but the hipped roof and lead clad-lantern remain.

From our position we could also see Dial Square. Footballers who played here became the foundation stone of one of Britain's premier soccer clubs, Arsenal F.C. Fans may also want to visit the Pullman Pub, close to Woolwich Arsenal Station and Beresford Square. This is where the Royal Arsenal Football Club decided to change their name to **Arsenal Football Club**.

Sir John Vanbrugh

Sir John Vanbrugh was the grandson of a refugee Flemish Huegenot sugar merchant. He was born in 1644, the fourth son and eldest survivor of a family of nineteen children. He made his money out of trading in sugar and molasses. By 1688 he had bought himself a commission in a foot regiment but resigned on learning that the regiment was being posted abroad.

Nevertheless he ended up in France where, during hostilities, he was arrested on a charge of spying and imprisoned in the Bastille. Eventually he was paroled on an exchange of prisoners and returned to England.

He took to writing plays and his first in 1696, The Relapse or Virtue in Danger, was a great success. His second, The Provoked Wife was also successful after it had been reviewed as 'bawdy'. By 1700 he had turned his hand to architecture, securing a commission through contacts in his regiment. He then designed his own house in London known as 'Goosepie House' which inspired Swift to write a poem about it.

With just two buildings under his belt, he managed to become the most important architect in the land by securing the government post of Controller of the Works. Having gained other key posts, Vanbrugh became an impresario, putting on plays and operas in London's Haymarket. However, success eluded him and he returned to architecture. By 1705 he had won the commission from Sir John Churchill to design Blenheim Palace which was to be a gift to Queen Anne.

However, at odds with Sarah Churchill, he abandoned the project. He married and built Vanbrugh Castle, "my Bastille" as a gift to his wife. His vision was to have his family housed in similar buildings on Vanbrugh Fields beside the castle. Today only the castle remains. His money dwindled and he died in 1726 leaving his widow to sell the castle which has since been converted into apartments.

"Lie heavy on him Earth. He laid many a load on thee"

Vanbrugh is believed to have made an important contribution to the architecture of the Arsenal, but much of the work previously attributed to him is now believed to be that of Hawksmoor.

Today the club is based in Highbury, North London. The buildings in the squares are attributed to Hawksmoor. Built between 1717 and 1720, only the entrance range remains of the complex of buildings which once existed around

Cannon barrels at Woolwich Arsenal

the two yards. Over the arch is a sundial. Hence the names Dial Arch and Dial Square. It's a must for Arsenal pilgrims.

The Arsenal, which sat on the banks of the Thames, also had its own railway and has been used for filming television programmes such as London's Burning. English Heritage are said to be building a Royal Artillery museum and a riverside walk.

Hawksmoor is also believed to have designed the Model Room on Tower Place while James Wyatt is credited with designing the Carriage Store in 1778 and, with Lewis Wyatt between 1806 and 1813, the Grand Store and New Laboratory Square.

Richard Lovelace – The Woolwich Cavalier

A key figure in the ***English Civil War*** which laid the basis for the British parliamentary system, Richard Lovelace, like generations of his family, was brought up in Woolwich. Born in 1618 and educated at Charterhouse School, he went on to become a soldier in the army fighting in Scotland in 1639.

When the Civil War broke out he had retired to Bethersden near Canterbury. However, a royalist, he was chosen to present the Kentish Petition demanding the restoration of the king's rights. For this Lovelace was imprisoned in the Gatehouse gaol at Westminster. There he wrote his poem, 'Althea'.

When love with unconfined wings hovers within my gates,
And my beloved Althea brings to whisper at the grates:
When I lie tangled in her hair and fetter'd to her eye,
The birds that wanton in the air knew no such liberty.
When flowing cups run swiftly round with no allaying Thames,
Our careless heads with roses bound, our heart, with loyal flames,
When thirsty grief in wine we steep, when health and thoughts
*   go free,*
Fishes which tipple in the deep know no such liberty.
When, like committed linnets, I with thrillen notes will sing,
The sweetness, mercy, majesty and glories of my king;
When shall I voice aloud how good he is, how great should be,
Enlarged wings, that curb the flood, know no such liberty.
Stone walls do not a prison make, nor iron bars a cage;
Minds innocent and quiet take that for an hermitage.
If I have freedom for my love and in my soul am free,
Angels alone that soar above enjoy such liberty.

The romantic prisoner was set free some months later and set about using his wealth to fund new troops for the royalist cause. He went to France and in 1646 formed a regiment. Two years later after being wounded during fighting at Dunkirk he returned to England, only to be imprisoned again, this time in the Peterhouse. He had fallen in love with a certain Lucy Sacheverall. In prison he wrote to his sweetheart, Lucastra:

> *"Tell me not, sweet, I am unkind, that from the nunnerie, Of thy*
> *chaste breast and quiet mind to wars and arms I fly.*
> *True, a new mistress now I chase, the first foe in the field; And*
> *with a stronger faith embrace a sword, a horse, a shield.*
> *Yet this inconstancy is such as you too shall adore; I could not*
> *love thee, dear, so much lov'd I not honour more."*

But his would-be mistress, hearing that he had been fatally wounded in France, married someone else, leaving Lovelace grief stricken.

Charles I was executed before Lovelace was released. Defeat, prison and grief had broken his wealth, health and heart. The rest of his life was spent in poverty and he died in squalor in Gunpowder Alley near Shoe Lane. He was buried in 1658 in St Brides church.

Riverside Woolwich

The location of Woolwich on the Thames gave the town an advantageous location. It was close enough to the Thames estuary to provide anchorage for shipping but far enough up river to afford security from attack by enemy ships.

As a result the location was deemed suitable for shipbuilding and later suitable for armaments stores. The **Dockyards** were built here, significantly altering life in the town. Today there are many reminders of Woolwich town's pre-eminence in maritime life. The Dockyards, when closed in the 60s, stretched from the ferry to Warspite Road.

We started along Defiance Walk beside the **Gun Drill Battery** overlooking the Thames. As it suggests, the battery was installed for training purposes in the 1840s. A little further inland still on Defiance Walk is the Clockhouse Community Centre. Built during the 1780s this building was once the Admiral Superintendent's house for the Royal Dockyards. The two storey brick building has seven bays, a hipped roof and a central clock tower. The two wooden porches by the central entrance are mid 19th century additions. Just down river from the Gun Drill Battery are the old Graving Docks built as a dry dock in 1841 and extended to a wet dock in 1848. Today it is only used for recreational fishing purposes.

Close to the pier on the north side of the river lies **North Woolwich Old Station Museum.** This former train station was built in 1845 in a Byzantine style using red brick with stone dressing. Today it is finished in cream and brown brick, having been restored to the condition it was likely to be in during 1910. The staff wear Edwardian costumes of the time and a railway engine is steamed on the first Sunday in the month. Admission is free.

Opening hours (tel 0207 474 7244) are Mon-Weds and Sat, 10am-5pm, Sundays and Bank Holidays, 2pm-5pm.

One way of getting back across the Thames from North Woolwich is to walk down and through the **Woolwich Foot Tunnel.** Besides the entry to the ferry terminal on Pier Road is a building topped with a glass dome which has a lift and stairwell to reach the tunnel. The tunnel was built between 1909 and 1912. The almost identical entrance south of the river is by Glass Yard. Talk inside and you'll find that it's a vibrant echo chamber and quite fun.

Down river of the Foot Tunnel entrance is **Riverside Walk** which is part of the river walk in the Greenwich Borough section of the Thames. The walk currently ends at, and offers a good view of, the Arsenal.

Woolwich Town

By Royal Charter proclaimed in 1619, James I granted the Lords of the Manor, the Maryon Wilsons of Charlton, the right to establish a market anywhere in Woolwich parish. They did so and **Woolwich Market** started in 1619 at the north end of what is now Beresford St, once known as Market Hill. In the 18th century it was moved to Beresford Square.

The Maryon-Wilsons were bought out by the local authority which now has, outside the City of London, the only Chartered Market in the capital of England.

Woolwich Free Ferry – the cheapest in the world

We took our car on the Woolwich Free Ferry from Woolwich Church St over to the north bank of the Thames. It's a good way to reach the M1 motorway.

There has been a ferry at Woolwich since at least 1308 when the ferry was a royal ferry subject to the control of Eltham Palace. Woolwich Free Ferry was begun in 1889, largely to link Woolwich with North Woolwich over the Thames. North Woolwich had acquired a rail station and the ferry allowed workers to reach the Arsenal.

The Free Ferry was opened in great pomp with a huge procession led by mounted police, marching bands and three companies of volunteer soldiers. Such was the excitement that during its first weekend the single ferry carried 25,000 passengers. In the past only passengers could travel on the ferries, with livestock travelling separately on 'horse rafts'.

With the advent of the paddle steamers all manner of man and beast could travel and the ferry became a veritable Noah's Ark. Cows, horses, sheep and pigs were common travellers and once a whole circus, elephants and all went aboard. One cunning Woolwich dog used the ferry to go and collect his regular bone from a butcher's shop on the north side.

Back then, the ferries, akin to Mississippi steamboats, were boarded from floating landing stages. The paddle steamers were replaced in 1963 and the landing stages were replaced in 1966 by the current terminals with steel-trussed ramps adjustable to a 30ft tidal range. The ferry trip is free and one of the oldest. Three ferries ply the river with two operating at one time.

Overlooking the square is Beresford Gate named after Lord Beresford who once headed the Arsenal. This imperial legacy was built from red brick with stone window surrounds in 1829 as the main entrance to the Arsenal. Now separated from the Arsenal and the perimeter wall it was further embellished in 1891.

Just off the square is **General Gordon Place**, once known as 'The Smoke Hole' because of a cutting that ventilated Woolwich Arsenal Station. The site was named to honour Gordon of Khartoum, the general who died in a British military campaign in the Sudan. The square had six pubs overlooking it and

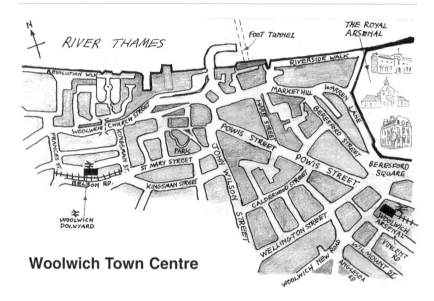

Woolwich Town Centre

sparked the construction of the Duke of Connaught Coffee House by the Temperance movement. On the site of the Coffee House is now a branch of Barclay's Bank. The last remaining pub became a mosque which itself closed in 1982.

Off Wilmount St is the **Old Tramshed**. Built in 1908 it is now a theatre reputed for excellent comedy nights. Woolwich New Road heads for the **Artillery Barracks** but on the left is another fine local church, **St Peter's** and the **Presbytery** on which work began in 1842. The church was designed by **AWN Pugin**, renowned as a Gothic revivalist he installed large buttresses and a huge English Gothic window. He built the Presbytery in 1849, with EW Pugin making additions in 1870. The stained glass was created by Wailes. The chancel and side chapel were later additions.

North of and parallel to Woolwich New Road is Wellington Street. The area bounded by John Wilson Street, Calderwood Street and Powis Street is the civic area of the town housing both the courts and **Greenwich University**. The civic area contains the **Old Town Hall** (1842), the classic-style Magistrates Court (1912), the public library (1901), **Woolwich Baths** (1894) and the distinctive ornamented **Woolwich Town Hall** (1903-1906). **Woolwich Public Hall** in Market Street is where we heard the fine **Royal Artillery Orchestra** play in concert for £5-£6.50 – worth a night out. Tickets are available from The Sales Unit (151 Powis St, tel 0208 317 8687).

Powis Street has two notable buildings of continental style. Elaborate Baroque decorations are used on number 12, Powis St while numbers 125-151 was built in 1902 to an Italian Renaissance style including a central dome. Number 151 is the home of **Citizen's Gallery** (tel 0208 855 3240) which stages a variety of art and educational exhibitions and has a daytime café.

'We're with the Woolwich'

The first home of the famous Woolwich Building Society was 145 Powis Street. Formed in 1847 it grew to become one of Britain's largest mutual savings and investments institution. Equitable House on Woolwich New Road became the society's headquarters in 1935. It is noted for its Edwardian Baroque style and mix of art deco motifs on the exterior which compliment the art deco banking hall. In 1989 the head office was moved to Bexleyheath.

We were heading back towards the pier head when we came across two interesting old cinemas. The **Gala Bingo Hall** opposite the ferry was built for the Granada Cinema chain in 1937. Art Nouveau in style, it was designed by Masey and Uren and Didock inspired. The spectacular interior was designed by Theodore Komisarjevsky from the Moscow Arts Theatre. Entrance can be gained by membership of the Bingo Hall but must be arranged the day before required. Opposite is another cinema put up in the same year, the George Cole designed, **Coronet Cinema**, once known as the Odeon (0208 854 2255) it has a cream façade and an interesting Art Deco interior.

Behind the Coronet on the rise is **St Mary Magdalene's church** in St Mary St. Like St Nicholas in Plumstead, the church tower was an important navigational aid for sailors on the river. Like Charlton church and St Nicholas, it is allowed to fly the Red Ensign on its flagstaff for ceremonial occasions. The church is built on sand and the old church is believed to have just slipped away. St Mary's was built in stock bricks by Deptford bricklayer, Matthew Spray, and completed in 1739. Two-storey arched windows and the plain west tower add to its attraction.

The interior has galleries on octagonal supports inter-spaced with Ionic columns and the nave ceiling is carefully vaulted. The chancel in yellow brick was an 1880s addition. Interestingly, the stained glass window at the west end of the south aisle records the death in 1878 of almost 600 people who drowned when the pleasure steamer, Princess Alice, sank in the Thames when off Tripcock Point, Woolwich.

Opening hours (tel 0208 316 4338), by appointment. **Disabled access**. Often overlooked in the churchyard is the great leonine monument to **Tom Cribb**, one of Britain's most famous prizefighters in the 19th century. Cribb died in poverty and was buried in the church in 1848.

WOOLWICH

Tom Cribb – The Bareknuckle Bruiser

Born into a family of farm labourers in 1781, Tom Cribb started his bareknuckle fighting career in the village of Hanham close to Bristol. A stocky 5ft 10inches and weighing 199lbs, his first recorded fights took place in 1805 when he beat Tom Blake and then Ikey Pigg. At the time bareknuckle fighting was illegal and often threatened by the intervention of those in authority. Nevertheless the ring brought fame to fighters, including freed American slave, Bill Richmond, who Cribb defeated earning the right to challenge another great rival, Jem Belcher for the championship.

In 1807, Bristol-born Belcher suffered a 35 minute battering at the hands of Cribb who was declared the winner after 41 rounds (a round was called when a fighter went to ground but many went down to avoid further punishment). After two successful defences of his title, Cribb met Belcher once more in 1809 on Epsom Downs where again he triumphed, this time within 31 rounds. The people sang:

> *"A true Briton from Bristol,*
> *A rum 'un to fib,*
> *He's the champion of England,*
> *His name is Tom Cribb."*

Bill Richmond had another freed slave in his camp, South Carolina-born Tom Molineaux. Molineaux was put up to challenge Cribb for his title at a time when most black slaves were considered by many to be no better than animals. Already a fighter in America, he arrived in England in 1809 and won several major fights.

The public was in for a great trial of strength between the two men. The great event took place on Copthall Common, Sussex, in 1810 and sparked one of prizefighting's most controversial and disgraceful incidents putting into shade today's scandals surrounding the first Lennox Lewis-Evander Holyfield show-down and the Mike Tyson ear biting incident.

The fight was brutal. By the 28th round Molineaux had forced Cribb to concede the round before promptly keeling over himself. By the 30th Molineaux was staggering, but still upright, while Cribb crawled around on the ground. Molineaux only needed to stay on his feet to be declared the victor. Suddenly one of Cribb's seconds, Joe Ward shouted out that Molineaux had a bullet in his fist. The incident caused so much commotion that by the time the umpires had decided that Ward's claim was false, Cribb had recovered and went on to win the contest in the 33rd round.

In the 1811 rematch, Molineaux had his jaw broken by Cribb, who won within 11 rounds. The two fighters became friends but at this point their fortunes separated. Molineaux died a broken man in Galway seven years later. Cribb

Map to Zero

For centuries, Greenwich has been the starting point for the exploration of the globe. Now, in this millennium year, the world is repaying the compliment by coming to Greenwich to explore its heritage and its attractions.

But there's more to Greenwich than clocks & domes ~ it's a vibrant, multicultural community that makes it a 'home from home' for the overseas student.

So, during your visit, why not phone us on:

(0181) 488 4848

and ask for a copy of our NEW PROSPECTUS to be posted to your home address... and think about coming back to us at zero longitude as an international student?

WOOLWICH COLLEGE & GREENWICH COMMUNITY COLLEGE

PROVIDING LIFELONG LEARNING FOR GREENWICH AND THE SOUTH EAST

Visit our web site at www.woolwich.ac.uk

became so famous that he was feted by king and commoner alike. In 1814 he performed his skills as the main entertainment for the Russian Czar and the King of Prussia.

In 1821 he was party to another piece of notoriety. When the Prince Regent (George IV) barred his unfaithful wife, Princess Caroline from his coronation, Cribb was hired along with 18 other fighters to assist the monarch. They were dressed as royal pages and ordered to prevent the supporters of the Princess from disrupting the ceremony in Westminster Abbey.

Cribb in his latter years lived with his son in Woolwich. The

Tom Cribb

St Mary's monument was erected on his death in 1848 when his fame remained such that nobody thought it necessary to list his deeds.

Religious Worship

Woolwich contains some of the most important non Anglican/Catholic places of worship in the borough. These include **Ramgarhia Sikh Temple** (tel 0208 854 1786, on Masons Hill, with **disabled access**, **open** 6am-7pm daily). This gurdwara of the **Ramgarhia Association** started life in 1889 as a Freemasons' Hall. Another gurdwara, **Woolwich Sikh Temple** (tel 0208 854 4233, **disabled access, open** 6am-7pm daily) is in Calderwood Street. The building was erected in 1816 for use by the Royal Artillery Garrison.

The biggest mosque in the borough is the red brick **Greenwich Islamic Centre** (tel 0208 855 0786, limited **disability access, open** till 11pm from 3.30pm in summer and 6am in winter). It has a school for children over six years old, provides facilities for the Islamic community and offers advice on housing, employment, health etc.

The Jewish community was finally granted its wish of a purpose-built synagogue in 1964. **The new Woolwich and District Synagogue** on Anglesea Rd, replaced the old one, formerly a Presbyterian hall, on the same site (tel 0208 854 3188, visits by appointment).

Plumstead

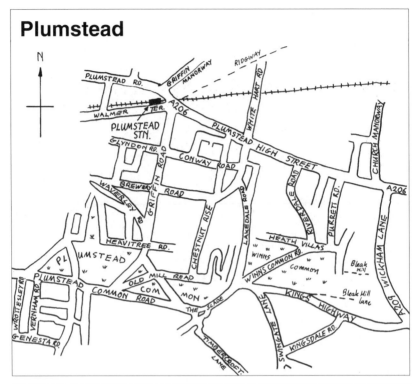

St Nicholas Church

PLUMSTEAD'S **Churches and Commons**

The discovery of a prehistoric burial mound on Plumstead Common and the many Celtic and Roman artefacts found indicate that settlements existed in the Plumstead area 2,000 years ago. Nevertheless, Plumstead remained a small village until the end of the 19th century because of its marsh land, Plumstead Marshes. Even today the level of the land around Plumstead is said to be falling by at least twelve inches every year while tidal levels are rising by 18 inches. Flood disasters often threatened.

Stow's Chronicles recorded in 1236, "About this time fell such abundance of raine in the space of two months that the Thames overflowed the banks causing the marshes about Wisbich (in other editions reported as Woolwich) to be on a Sea, whereupon the boats and other small vessels were carried to the stream, so that besides cattle, the greatest number of men, women and children inhabiting these parts were drowned: In the great Palace of Westminster men did row with wherries in the middest of the hall and they rode on horseback to their Chambers."

The malaria ridden marshes were only used for gun practice until they were drained in the mid 19th century. However the small fishing and farming village has clearly existed in some form since Roman times. Buried in **St Nicholas Church** are the bones of a Roman woman from 300AD found with luxurious items in a coffin. The coffin is now in Maidstone Museum.

The first record of Plumstead comes from a deed held in the British Museum and issued by King Edgar of England, considered to be the first king of all England. Edgar had become king in 959 at the age of 16. His coronation, which took place in Bath, wasn't until 973, two years before his death in 975. Edgar, by the deed of 960, granted "to St Augustine, Apostle of the English, and to the brethren of his holy monastery.......the four ploughlands called Plumstede, with the consent of Dunstan, Archbishop, and of my nobles."

In the 6th century, **Augustine**, on a mission to convert the heathen English, had landed at Thanet, founding an abbey outside the walls of Canterbury City on a site donated by **King Ethelred**. The Abbey of St Augustine therefore took lordship of all Plumstead and the adjacent Wickham.

In the decades prior to the arrival of the Norman invaders of William the Conqueror, the Manor grew prosperous and a target for avaricious local nobles. However, seizing the Manor from the church would prove to be a poisoned chalice. Godwin, Earl of Kent, seized the Manor from the Abbey presenting it to

PLUMSTEAD

his son, Tostan. Edward the Confessor subsequently retook the Manor from Tostan, handing the lands back to the Abbey.

When Edward died, Tostan reclaimed the Manor, only to be killed by his brother **King Harold**, who took the land in 1066. Unluckily for him, William and his Norman armies marched into town. King Harold was slain at the **Battle of Hastings**. The land, together with Eltham, was then given to Odo, Bishop of Bayeaux and Earl of Kent, who in turn was ordered by his brother-in-law, Archbishop Lanfranc and William I in a charter to return the Manor to the Abbey.

The **Normans** enriched the Abbey which became the most important Benedictine Abbey in England and said in Europe to be only second to Monte Cassino. Pledged to the work ethic of Opus Dei, the monks gained respect for their deeds in the area.

Covering only 120 acres, Plumstede (as it was then known) and Wickham is hard to imagine, but given much of the area was Thames marshland, the plough-lands probably referred to the cultivable areas on chalk spurs emanating from the rise where Plumstead's commons lie. The parish was bounded by the Thames, Nightingale Brook (there's still a Nightingale Vale) and up to Woodlands Farm on Shooters Hill. Mediaeval documents recorded 'Plumstede' as a well ordered self-sufficient farming and fishing community equipped with its manor, clergy, steward, bailiff, beadle, prison and gallows. The population made their living by various means including fishing. The church in Plumstead has always been dedicated to St Nicholas, patron saint of sailors and fisher-men. Ancient records regarding the parish record rules of how salmon and stur-geon should be transported to the court at Whitehall. Eels and lampreys were among the catches and whales were often found stranded. In 1313, the Lord Abbot of St Augustine's was prosecuted "for that he did take a certain whale in the river Thames of his lands in Plumstead of the value of 40 shillings and did retain the said whale for his own profit."

PLUMSTEAD

Farming was common and Plumstead was the place where the cherry tree and the pippin apple first grew in Britain. The marshes also provided for plenty of bird life, drawing herons, swans, geese and ducks. A trade grew in plucking bird feathers to provide for quill pens and the fashionable plumes of the lords and ladies in London. History does not record whether the name, Plumstead, comes from the plumes or plums of the villagers.

The marshland was often subject to flooding and the gentry moved up on the slope below Plumstead Common. Despite floods and pestilence, the village prospered until the 16th century, and the time of the Dissolution of the Monasteries and the Reformation under Henry VIII. St Augustine's Abbey was dissolved in 1538 and in 1539 **Henry VIII** granted the Manor to his agent, Sir Edward Boughton of Burwash (Burrage) Court. The name Burwash derived from Lord Bartholomew de Burghesh of Plumstead, a Norman noble of whom the poet Chaucer was said to be a descendent.

The king's advisor, Thomas Cromwell, sent Vaughan to draw up an inventory of property under the control of the Abbey but while he could list the lands of the monastery, he was unable to discover the other lands of the Manor due to public resentment. Vaughan reported to Cromwell that "the people here are so obstinate that they were four days in finding a man to show the lands in Plumstead belonging to the Manor". The Plumstead people are a much friendlier bunch today.

By the mid 19th century the marsh land still dominated the area and Plumstead remained a small farming and fishing community. Only with the massive expansion of the Arsenal, and the need to house its workforce and build servicing industries, did Plumstead become what it is today. The rail station opened in 1859. Up on the rise the village still retains its semi-rustic character.

St Nicholas Church

We discovered St Nicholas church by St Nicholas Gardens park almost by chance, this historic building being excluded from the normal tourist trail through the borough. It shouldn't be because it relates part of the fascinating history of Plumstead and its surrounds. The church lies just off the main road allowing us to park close by. It may not have the grace or uniformity of St Alfege's or the other popular churches of the area but its patchwork creation testifies to the common fate of many historic churches whereby great plans ran out of money quicker than the architectural passions of the period.

In that sense St Nicholas is very reminiscent of those old Italian churches stuffed with recycled materials, history hiding in nooks and crannies or hanging on to a wall or ceiling. Many old window surrounds were blocked up rather than removed, entrances were covered over and, to the rear of the church one can see vestiges of the previous fan vaulting.

The church grounds are littered with ancient gravestones and sarcophagi and so raised above the level of the church that one has to descend to the entry. The cemetery once included St Nicholas Gardens, now a small park with play facilities for children. 40,000 burials had taken place in the grounds up until 1890 and new tombs had to be placed on top of the others, also explaining the uneven ground close to the church.

This site saw previous human activity as evidenced by the finds of 2nd century Roman coins in the burial ground. The church is believed to have been founded in 950AD probably as a wooden edifice. The first stone and rubble church is believed to have been built in the 12th century, including the south and west walls of the south aisle in river stone. There are two splayed windows from this time. These windows such as that above the porch would have let in a small amount of light and would have been glass-free but filled with hay or straw in winter to keep out the cold. The stain glass picture in the window above the porch is modern, depicting St Nicholas as Bishop of Myra. In the legend he rescued three children from an evil butcher during a period of an acute meat shortage.

Most of the form of the current building dates to the 13th century when the church was expanded. The south transept was built at this time though reduced in 1960. The east wall still stands and the chancel with its small arch was built wider than the nave. The columns of the south aisle date to this period delimiting the then size of the church. The work was clearly quite rough as testified by the south wall and the attempts to fit various shapes into the walls in the door surrounds. In 1958 workmen found a 13th century chisel, presumably lost by a workmen and buried in the wall between the south aisle and the west wall of the transept. A unique find, it now sits in the Science Museum in South Kensington.

The work is dated to 1230 and was never completed. It is assumed that this was due to the great flood catastrophe that followed. The next century saw little but the blocked Gothic doorway adjacent to the current entrance. It was discovered just days before the newly restored church was due to open in 1907.

The 15th century saw the north wall of the nave replaced by the current 15th century arcade of four bays and the aisle thrown out to the north. A door was cut into the 12th century west wall of the church and the pivots on which the door was hung can still be seen on the exterior. The inner ring of the arch on the arcades between the south aisle and the nave came from the 13th century chancel arch.

A special feature of the church is its splendid tower, first built into the church in 1664 by Churchwarden Gossage in late Gothic style. Clasping buttresses are carried up as turrets and topped off with battlements. It was a great achievement following the time of Civil War and the Restoration in which Charles II suppressed the Protestant Prayer Book and issued his own version. Gossage is buried beneath the paving in the churchyard as is William Bennett, Bishop of Cloyne who died in 1820.

Above the tower is a flagstaff with a story. Being close to the Thames on rising ground, the church tower and flagstaff had been used for many years as a beacon for ships arriving in London. They were also used by the Gentleman Cadets of the Royal Artillery for siting and calculating distances on their rangefinders. In the late 19th century the flagstaff was destroyed in a storm. The War Department contacted the vicar of St Nicholas requesting that it be replaced. The vicar replied that they would do so if the War Department paid. The government finally agreed in 1884 to loan the church a new flagstaff cut from a Russian fir tree shipped to the Arsenal, weighing half a ton and standing 30ft high. The bell tower consists of four bells. Three of the bells were cast in 1686 and the fourth in 1790. They are tuned to A, B, C sharp and D minor but poor

St Nicholas Church

workmanship in their hanging means they can only be chimed without turning on their stocks.

The creation of the tower coincided with not only the turbulent times of the Restoration but also the battle to increase the profits of British manufacturers and merchants. The church register in 1678 records that a Mary Griffin was buried, 'in woolen'. Many entries like this followed. The government sought to protect the English wool trade against the threat of Dutch wool and linen and in 1666 issued a law on burials. By Act of Parliament they decreed that all burials must be in cloth or clothing made wholly of wool. When this was largely ignored they issued a new Act in 1669 requiring that an affidavit must be produced certifying that the dead were buried in 'woolen only' within eight days of internment.

The register also records the burial of John and George Robards, killed in 1688 when they fell into a crater created by a granado shell on Shooters Hill.

In 1702, a London merchant, Nathaniel Maxey, bought the Manor House and the estate of Burrage from the Burrages, then known as Burwashs. The Congleton silk pioneer manufacturer, James Pattison, married Mary Maxey and thus took over the Burrage estate. The Register records how the Pattisons not only took over the estate but also its children. In 1781, it was recorded, "agreed that all girls at the height of 4ft at the age of six years are to be bound out apprentice to Nathaniel Pattison Esquire at the silk mills at Congleton in Cheashire to be found with two suites of cloaths, a working suite and a Hollyday suite".

A gravestone destroyed during the 1939-45 war told a similar story. In 1812,

PLUMSTEAD

James Darling, a ten year old cartridge boy in the Arsenal, was caught stealing cherries. His captor beat him to death but was acquitted for the crime. The boy's epitaph read:

> **"Weep not for me, my parents dear,**
> **There is no witness wanted here,**
> **The hammer of Death was given to me,**
> **For eating the Cherries off the tree.**
> **Next morning Death was to me so sweet,**
> **My blised Jesus for to meet.**
> **He did ease of me my pain,**
> **And I did join his holy train.**
> **The cruel one his death can't shun,**
> **For he must go when his glass is run.**
> **The horrors of Death isure to meet,**
> **And tak his trial at the Judgement seat."**

The growth of artillery and the Arsenal changed life in Plumstead. The occasional stray bombardment and huge explosions also changed the church. In 1875 the vicar petitioned for bombardment damage but two huge explosions severely damaged the church in 1907 prompting restoration. More damage was created by proximity to Woolwich in 1945 when a German V2 rocket dropped in the burial ground, blowing off part of the roof. The vicar taking us around commented: "The roof's been more off than on in the last century."

Many who served in the Royal Artillery and Engineers are buried in the grounds, including Sergeant Major John Gillies who died in 1858. He was the last serving soldier from the Royal Artillery who had fought in Napoleon's debacle at Waterloo. Also buried here is Sir William Green, Bar RE who designed and built the Gibraltar defences between 1761 and 1779. Just in time. For the Rock then had to withstand a four year siege during which he was Chief Engineer. The said nephew of economist Adam Smith, author of the "Wealth of Nations", he was promoted to Chief Engineer of Great Britain.

Inside, the church had a rarefied and sombre atmosphere. We were visiting during Lent. As this was an Anglican church, the service retains much of the Catholic tradition. Catholic-raised Muriel was more at home with the various terms used for the services than I was, having been educated in the services of mainstream Church of England. Nevertheless, it was fascinating to see a Protestant church with all the trappings of Catholicism. The vicar was amenable, informative, and pleased to welcome tourists and visitors.

An interesting feature in the Lady Chapel is the **Hanging Pyx** beneath the baldachino above the altar. The Pyx reserves the Blessed Sacrament assuring worshippers that they are in the presence of Christ. Few have been used since mediaeval times and the church had to go to Southwark Consistory Court in 1960 to petition its legality. Also of note is the wonderful wooden ceiling of the Lady Chapel in the old tradition of an upturned keel, an allusion to Christ the Fisherman. **Visits** by appointment (tel 0208 854 0461), Sunday Service 11am. **Disabled access.**

Up the Rise to Plumstead Common

From the flats we climbed up the hill past rows of council houses to the larger houses on Burrage Rd, so named because it led to the old Manor house. The top of the hill with its pretty houses is where the more affluent would live. Local historian, WT Vincent once lived here. Soon we were on Plumstead Common Rd and into St Margaret's Grove. We passed the **Swanivayam Hindu temple**.

We arrived at the site of the elegant **Bramblebury House**. Constructed in the 18th century it was built on a site once owned by Charles I. Queen's College, Oxford became the Lords of the Manor but in 1859 the fine Georgian house became a vicarage and, with vicars in residence till 1966, is known as The Old Vicarage. Today it is being restored but our visit at least gave us great views over the Thames plain.

Next stop was **Plumstead Common**. It is one of the village's three open spaces, the others being Winn's Common and the Slade. All rest at the top of a 200ft plateau running parallel to the Thames and pocketed with dramatic combs and valleys. These inroads into the plateau were thought to have been made during the Ice Age when tundra ice and seeping water worked away eroding geological faults in the rock below. Near Lakedale Rd one can see the exposed shiny pebbles of the Blackheath beds of rock. The land here is populated by scattered scrubs and the occasional oak, sycamore, elder and birch trees.

Beside Kings Highway on **Bleak Hill** one finds sessile oaks, birches, ash and alders looking down on holly, aspen and goat willow shrubs. One flower worth looking out for is hedge mustard. Rub it in your hand and it exudes a strong smell of garlic. Others common here include bluebells, cow parsley, rose-bay and willow herb.

Plumstead Common has natural deposits of sand and these were dug out for making glass in the Arsenal, creating dips and furrows in the landscape. The common was taken over for artillery firing practice until the late 19th century. As it was only later restored to the people, it remained quite rural.

Further on east we came to **Bird's Nest Hollow** near Blendon Terrace, a dip in the common with a rock studded pit. At the heart of the dip are the **puddingstone** boulders which were deposited during the Ice Age and look like christmas puddings. It's a lovely part of the Common.Overlooking is the attractive clay brick built 1856 school of St Margarets on St Margarets Grove.

The Battle of Plumstead Common

After Henry VIII had seized Lesnes Abbey, the lands of the Manor were at his disposal. Plumstead Common was given to the King's Clerk, Sir Edward Boughton. The Boughton family kept the land until 1656 when it was bought by John Michel of Richmond. Richmond bequeathed the Common to Queen's College, Oxford. As Lords of the Manor, Queen's College, held the Common in the 19th century.

Their stewardship by then had allowed the common to dete-riorate to such a state that a local report described the Common as, "a mangy spot on the dog's back." Many small pockets of land were being encroached upon. By 1874 the college had allowed the common to be fully appropriated as a riding and drill school for the troops based at Woolwich. The Common had long been a source of recreation for the villagers but the college declared their wish to lease the area on a per-manent basis to the military, and erected fences blocking the traditional rights of way.

On July 1st, 1876 Commons Protection League member and friend of Karl Marx, John de Morgan, led a protest march from the gates of the Arsenal to the Common. Their the protesters removed the fences preventing the rights of way and left singing, 'Rule Britannia'. That night the authorities re-erected the fences. The protesters returned and once more pulled down the fences but this time, stone throwing, burning and rioting followed.

PLUMSTEAD

Edwin Hughes, the local Vestry Clerk lived on the edge of the Common and, despite John de Morgan not being present at the common, had de Morgan charged with incitement to riot. Of the four people tried at the court only de Morgan was found guilty. The agitator was sentenced to one month in prison and ordered to pay a £50 fine. His imprisonment sparked new protests and 20,000 people turned up at the Common to watch an effigy of Hughes being hung and then burnt.

The protests eventually led to victory and in 1877 the Common was placed in municipal hands being bought by the Metropolitan Borough of Works.

We arrived at another part of the commons used for gun fights and the scene of protests, near the Ship Inn. Behind the green on Old Mill Rd stands the lemon coloured **Old Mill Pub** which has been a public house since the time of Charles II. It is part of the 18th century Old Windmill, a smoke mill used until the 1850s. In 1848 the mill ceased to grinding wheat and turned to selling alcohol. Around are plenty of cherry orchards, in the middle tumuli and the first ever open air paddling pool.

Below the shops we could see alms houses erected in 1890. Extremely decorative, they had fascinating facades reminiscent of Renaissance architecture. On the Slade by Warwick Terrace common we looked down to where the landscape is spliced by a huge dried up river valley from a coomb gouged out during the Ice Age. Steps lead down to a lake. On the way down were fir trees and bushes which locals still have the right to cut for their fires.

Between King's Highway and Lakedale, the common's easterly end is known as **Winn's Common**. It is a beautiful part of Plumstead, a vast pasture flanked by small terraced cottages and guaranteed to make the area fashionable again. The central part of Winn's was the site of what is believed to have been a **Bronze Age burial mound** and later the centre was used for horse and gun carriage practice.

The Slade overlooks the Thames and though at first site it looks flat, has great dips. We approached the edge of a coomb. The dried up river valley with its steep sides occupied by trees stretched down to the plain below. A stepped path offered a pleasant walk through **Great Bartlett Woods** down to houses on the valley bottom.

Below was the Arsenal, the site of an old workhouse. On Riverdale Road we came across **Belmarsh Prison**. Many died escaping the old prison hulks and were buried on the marshes. Beyond were the twin towers of the Northern Docks and above a plane dipped its nose to land at the City Airport.

Greenwich Borough Museum at 232, Plumstead High Street is on the upper floor above the public lending library. We entered and were amazed by the compact display illustrating the history of the area from the Thames to Eltham. Stuffed birds of prey, the head of a young crocodile and an armadillo greeted us as we climbed the stairs. Old truncheons, some worn down to a frightening extent sat in a display cabinet with other memorabilia from the village's old police station.

As we went in there were examples of heraldry from Eltham Palace including that of Prince John of Eltham born to King Edward II and Queen Isabella in 1316 at the palace. He died at 20 years of age in the palace. The museum has many artefacts from the Neolithic Era including Middle Stone Age flint tools from Shooters Hill, and flint instruments including axe heads and daggers of the Beaker folk, a people who brought with them knowledge of the use of metal in

Lesnes Abbey ruins

1800 B.C. Finds indicating the early use by the Romans of the road to Dover, include 1st century earthenware Roman pottery from Shooters Hill.

Bronze Age gold bracelets were found at Bexley and are displayed here, along with finds from Woolwich and the Arsenal. Also on display are Roman artefacts found along the Roman road which ran through Plumstead, and finds from a burial ground found beneath Dial Square in the Arsenal. Coins found beneath Plumstead High St from the 1st to 4th centuries bearing the heads of Emperors Claudius, Constantine, Vespasian, Anthony, Aurelius and Constantius II are also on show.

The display cabinets with model reconstructions of Bronze Age, Roman and Anglo Saxon life were particularly useful and informative, giving a picture of what life might have been like in the borough between 1,000 and 2,000 years ago.

Pottery was on display from the court of Greenwich born Henry VIII along with plenty of other artefacts from this era and pictorial displays of the area's later history. A few of the rare pieces including 15th century panels rescued from Eltham Palace are on show with detail of the palace's history.

The museum holds a fun **Saturday Club** for children with varied themes including football, and Florence Nightingale in which local actors and actresses often participate. Museum (0208 855 3240) **opening hours** are Tues-Sat 10am-1pm, 2pm-5pm, Mon 2pm-7pm, Wednesdays and Sundays closed.

THAMESMEAD **Monks and Marshes**

Abbey Wood train station marks the southern point where the Thames marshes end and the river cliff begins. Just east of Abbey Wood station and off Abbey Wood Rd lie the splendid ruins of Lesnes Abbey. We had taken the car and found that we could park on New Rd and within 100 yards of the ruins. The Abbey, which is set in Abbey Wood, is the best place to start when visiting Thamesmead. Not only is it part of the story of this eastern and most northern part of the borough but it marks another point in the history of England.

Lesnes Abbey

In 1170 when Henry II was on the throne, the Archbishop of Canterbury was Thomas A Beckett. As Archbishop Beckett wielded enormous power and influence and King Henry saw Beckett as a nuisance. "Rid me of this turbulent priest," he is said to have declared. Richard de Lucy as Chief Justiciar of England took his highness King Henry seriously. So did others in the king's coterie and four knights set upon Beckett and stabbed him to death in Canterbury Cathedral.

When he heard that the assassins had succeeded, the king realised that he'd made a terrible mistake. De Lucy, who had fought in the Crusades, agreed with his sire. In penance the warrior had Lesnes Abbey built and retired from service in 1178. The abbey was still being built when he moved in during 1179. De Lucy died within months and was buried in the grounds. The beneficiaries of de Lucy's penance were the monks of the Order of St Augustine. This powerful order also possessed large parts of Plumstead and dominated the area.

Known as the 'Black Canons' because of their black habits, the monks set about reclaiming the Lesnes marshland north of the abbey and beside the Thames. They are credited with having built the first river wall to prevent flooding at this point on the river.

We wandered around the carefully preserved ruins of the abbey. The site is quite beautiful with simple but neat ornamental gardens and the massed trees of Abbey Wood rising on mounds to the south. Much of the abbey has been reduced to low walls and foundations but the sections of the abbey ruins are well signposted making for an interesting visit.

Abbey Wood was controlled by the Black Canons and stretched as far east as Erith. Sweet chestnut trees used to dominate the forest and can still be found

THAMESMEAD

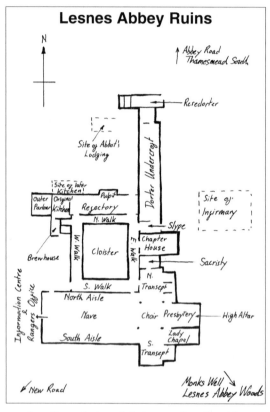

Lesnes Abbey Ruins

N

Abbey Road
Thamesmead South

Reredorter

Site of Abbot's
Lodging

Porter Undercroft

Site of later
Kitchen

Outer Parlour | Original Kitchen | Pulpit

Refectory

N. Walk

Site of
Infirmary

Slype

W. Walk

Cloister

E. Walk

Chapter House

Brewhouse

Sacristy

N.
Transept

S. Walk

North Aisle

Information Centre
& Rangers Office

Nave

Choir Presbytery High Altar

South Aisle

Lady Chapel

S.
Transept

New Road

Monks Well
Lesnes Abbey Woods

today with the many oak trees. Visitors in spring can wade through 20 golden acres of daffodils or come later to see them replaced by an equally extensive carpet of bluebells. The hills on the east side of the abbey are also noted for the fossils of shells, mammals, reptiles and fish found in the underlying rock known as the Blackheath Beds.

We entered the abbey via its church, which was so large that it could have been mistaken for a cathedral. De Lucy clearly wished to display his power and munificence. For the surrounding lands were sparsely populated and the Black Canons in residence thought to be few in number. Nevertheless it is known that the abbey was grand enough to be visited by King Edward I, Edward the Conqueror, on his way to Canterbury in 1300. We could identify the aisles, the transepts and bases on which columns once stood.

Adjacent and to the north side of the church we found the cloister where the friars would have sat in contemplation on a balmy Kent day having just emerged from a session at the chapter house opening on to the east side of the cloister. The chapter house was so called because here the monks would listen each day to a chapter of the holy scriptures.

On the south side of the cloister lies the refectory where the monks would wine and dine. Close by is the kitchen. A Gothic doorway identifies the age of the abbey as do the narrow slits which served as windows whilst keeping out the winter cold and the summer heat. North of the chapter house lie the ruins of the dormitory whose limited size gives a clue as to how many monks worked the abbey.

THAMESMEAD

The abbey is believed to have been built from Normandy stone but on the outer walls we could see many blocks of flint. These were probably picked up from the river that used to flow down from the hills to the south. The river, which was tidal at its estuary, long ago silted up and its path is now followed by Wickham Lane to the west. One task the monks had to perform in 1381 relates to the river. It is recorded that a group of Poll Tax rebels from Erith arrived at the Abbey on their way to join **Wat Tyler** at Blackheath. They demanded a boat from the canons so that they could cross the river. The friars duly obliged and the rebels took their place at Blackheath in the great **Peasants' Revolt.**

The Abbey prospered by reclaiming the marshlands now known as Thamesmead. Farms were established and covered much of the area. In 1525 the abbey would be hit by the beginning of another great national event. Henry VIII was about to rein in the power of the country's churches. His ally was Cardinal Wolsey and Wolsey's agent, Dr William Burbank took possession of the abbey and closed it down. The abbey's income was used to set up Christ's College, Cambridge. Thereafter came the great events of the **Dissolution of the Monasteries**, a royal revolution against the power of the Franco-Spanish dominated Catholic European empire.

From then on the abbey would be used as a farm. By 1630 it was described as being a ruin, its stones being carried off for use on other buildings. One of the effects of the closing of the monastery was an end to regular maintenance of the river wall that protected the farms on the marsh. By 1537 the walls were so dilapidated that they were breached by the Thames and 2,000 acres were flooded never to be fully reclaimed till 70 years later.

In 1563 an Act of Parliament allowed exiled Italian theologian and engineer Giacomo Aconzio to reclaim part of the land. The act stated that he must, "during the term of four years next following, to inne, fence and win the said ground, or any parcel of them." In return Aconzio would have, "the moiety of the lands so won for his charges." Within two years he had embanked a quarter of the land and by 1587, three quarters of it.

The flood walls were still occasionally breached and without proper drainage much of the area remained malaria-ridden swampland until the middle of the 19th century.

Wilson's Thamesmead

With the growth of the Royal Arsenal at Woolwich, those parts of the Lesnes marshes which were not farmland were taken over by the military. Here in the desolate marshes army engineers would test out new weapons of war and store explosives. One old firing wall still remains. The land was used as test tracks for new vehicles and tanks would be driven to destruction to assess their durability. Many buildings were put up for military purposes and canals and ponds

THAMESMEAD

Thamesmead

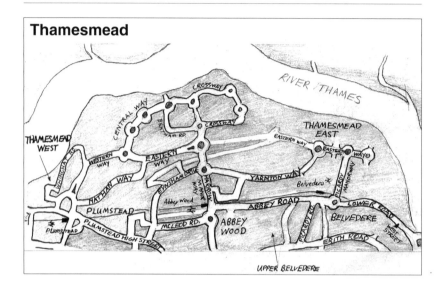

created. Otherwise the farmers, gypsies, fish, ducks and geese would be left alone. Only the area off the flood plain around Abbey Wood and Bostall Wood was developed.

The Thames broke its banks again in 1953 and caused widespread devastation on the marshes. By 1966 development of the marsh had been slow. That all changed with the arrival of Harold Wilson's reforming Labour Government of 1964/70. Keen to rehouse the tens of thousands of people in the capital still living in pre-war slums, the government embarked on a major house building programme. New housing estates would be constructed across the country, particularly in the south east. Polluted, grimy, bomb-damaged, overcrowded streets would be replaced by greenfield sites on the edge of the cities with plenty of space for recreation.

Thamesmead was built as part of the new Labour vision. Although it was aimed to provide homes for 60,000 people, the government never achieved its target. They also constructed lakes and parks and left plenty of open space making Thamesmead a pleasant place for open air recreation. The **marshes** are definitely worth visiting by those who like walking, fishing, watching wildlife or boating. ***Thamesmead Town Centre Clock*** is an 18th clock and cupola. The clock once stood in Deptford Dockyard but was moved to the town in 1982 to create an attractive central feature. The clock retained its original movement dating back to 1782. Subsequently it was found to be so irregular that the movement was disconnected from the four faces and an electrically operated self-correcting motor installed. Deptford still awaits the return of its clock.

What Labour could not do is create a reasonable shopping area. We could only find one café, in the Safeway's supermarket. Film buffs may be attracted to the area. It was here that Stanley Kubric's celebrated violent cult movie, Clockwork Orange, was made.

Thamesmead's Plumstead Marshes

It may be confusing to visitors but Plumstead Marshes are today part of Thamesmead district. On the western edge of Thamesmead Town, the marshes begin to the north of Plumstead High Street, immediately after Belmarsh Prison, which sits in Dickensian fashion in the middle of the swampland. Then Western Way cuts through the middle dividing into Central Way which heads to Thamesmead town centre and Eastern Way which passes by Birchmere Lake.

Despite the effects of past pollution from the Arsenal, the marshes have developed into an excellent haven for wildlife. At the east end known as Tripcock Park, elder bushes dominate the scrubland, though tree planting has given the area a far less desolate appearance. Kestrels can at times be seen hovering overhead as the rabbits which once dominated 'The Warren' run for cover.

Between the rabbits and the kestrels, the air in summer is dominated by **butterflies.** They are attracted by the plentiful nettles said to thrive on nitrogen-rich soil left behind by the explosives factories. These stinging nettles are especially attractive to the red admiral, the peacock, the small tortoiseshell and the comma when in their larval stage.

The comma butterfly is said to be particularly interesting as it is so difficult to spot. As a caterpillar its black and white markings and spines make it appear like bird dropping. As an adult its ragged edged mottled brown wings ensure it can be mistaken for a dead leaf, and the white underside of the hindwings for a glimmer of daylight through a torn hole. Summer visitors from abroad include the painted lady and the rare clouded yellow varieties.

The ground is spattered by a great variety of grasses dependent on the local environments. The tops of the banks have Yorkshire fog, crested dog's tail, fiorin, tall fescue, couch grass, feverfew, hoary wagwort, hardheads, ox-eye daisy, wild carrot, scarlet pimpernel, stinking groundsel, viper's bugloss and bristly ox-tongue, just to name a few of the more exotically named species. Mosses, ferns and lichens denote the old pathways once trodden by the Arsenal workers.

South east of Tripcock Park is a large area of **wetlands** with **reed beds**, drainage dykes and lagoons. Along the waterways one can find typical marshland flora; reed, great reedmace, great hairy willow herb, gipsy-wort, figwort, bulrush and celery-leaved crowfoot. Other plants survive in the waters; water plantain, curled, horned and fennel-leaved pondweeds, and hornwort. Above them are the silver birch trees, common to Thamesmead, and swooping around are herons and kingfishers attracted by the plentiful supply of fish.

North east of Tripcock Park lies the area once dominated by the banks and moats of the **Twin Tumps**. The Tumps were constructed to allow for the storage of explosives. Today they are surrounded by a woodland of silver birch. The moats have filled with water and the reed beds attract moorhens while reed and sedge warblers breed in the shelter. Herons and kingfishers are also dominant here where they find fish in abundance. Pathways take ramblers through the woods and beside them one can find patches of white mullein and birdsfoot-trefoil.

At the north east end lies **Thamesmere Extension**, an artificial lake which nevertheless attracts many species of wildfowl including snipes, redshanks, coots, shovelers, moorhens, mallard and tufted ducks, black-headed gulls and cormorants. The lakes at Birchmere and Gallions also attracts these species, as well as other birds common to Thamesmead include the common sandpiper, the spotted flycatcher and the lesser whitethroat.

Further east on the edge of **Erith Marsh** and beside Yarnton Way lies **Southmere Lake**, the largest in Thamesmead. **The Lakeside Centre** is a popular for location for **yachting, sailboarding, canoeing** and **fishing**, and has a popular **restaurant** and **bar**. We counted some dozen yachts in the water on a weekday evening. They were accompanied by thirty or so ducks as we sat in the leafy area beside the lake watching young children feed the pigeons. It was all as Prime Minister, Harold Wilson had imagined, with tower blocks looking over the water allowing the people of Thamesmead to enjoy the green pastures and silvery waters.

North of the lake, across Eastern Way lies Crossway park. Another large stretch of parkland, it includes tennis courts and the home of **Thamesmead Football Club**. **Thamesmere Leisure Centre** (tel 0208 311 1119) on Thamesmere Drive has modern swimming pools, a fitness room, keep fit studio, creche, sauna and sunbed suite.

THAMESMEAD

THE MILLENNIUM DOME **Greenwich**

At Stratford, north of the Thames, we took the tube on the ***Jubilee Line*** to the new ***North Greenwich station*** beside the Dome. The Dome was not yet open and the train was eerily empty. Arriving at North Greenwich, the station was similarly deserted but it gave us a chance to appreciate what is probably London's most attractive tube station.

Recently opened the station is an elegant mass of sea blue, with blue sloping columns, silvery grey pipes and square port holes. Ascending via the escalator and walking along the wide walkways was like entering a huge ocean liner. Muriel only saw the station when leaving the Dome. As she descended into the cavernous blue she remarked that she felt as if she was going beneath the sea. Try it yourself and you'll appreciate the enigmatic designs of the architects.

Exiting the station we saw the Dome on our right. For the first time we were seeing it close up. With all the road and building works going on around the impression was truly futuristic. Yellow antennae burst out of the Dome's fabric roof. Here was a Martian spaceship captured by the air force. It was a fitting description, for the Millennium Dome is truly a wonder of the modern world. Indeed it is one of only three buildings that can be detected with the naked eye from outer space.

The Dome is the biggest dome structure in the world, has the biggest roof and biggest fabric structure of any building in the world and will house the largest number of visitors' attractions in any building on earth. The base area could accommodate twenty five Taj Mahals. The masts lean three times more than the Leaning Tower of Pisa and are fourty metres taller. The roof may be made of fabric but experts say that while it can be cut with a knife it is strong enough to land a jumbo jet on. Don't worry. We were assured that there are no plans to perform this feat in the near future. We climbed to the gantry way above the floor of the dome and looked down on what looked like a tiny model of a red London bus. Except the bus was no toy. It was simply dwarfed by the size of the Dome. In fact, the huge structure is capable of holding around 18,000 buses. So too could almost four billion cans of lager, enough for the whole of Britain to party for a fortnight.

There has been much debate about the value of the Dome project. Apart from being a landmark in engineering and architectural achievement which will impact on construction design for the coming decades, it also houses exhibits and displays some of the most incredible advances in technology which will impact on the future of civilisation.

MILLENNIUM DOME

Personally, I entered the Dome as a doubter. From North Greenwich station the structure had seemed surprisingly undaunting. However by the time I had walked around the various exhibits under construction and passed into the central arena to peer upwards, I was amazed at the enormity and ingenuity of this project.

That the Millennium Dome, as the high point of Britain's celebration of the Millennium, should be based in the borough of Greenwich is fitting not only because Greenwich is home to the prime meridian and world time. A thousand years ago the borough was a key staging post for the travellers who would set out on their pilgrimage to Rome celebrating the 1000th anniversary of the birth of Jesus Christ. Back then, Europe was emerging from the virtual barbarism of the Dark Ages. Pilgrims would travel by foot, horse and cart along the Watling Road to Dover then cross the English Channel to continue their trek to the holy shrines. Their journey was perilous and threatened by robbers, storms and sickness.

In 1000 AD only the gods could fly, inhabit the heavens and communicate with each other over 1000s of miles. Today, modern pilgrims can reach Rome in a matter of hours and, BT and Vatican permitting, can see and even speak to the Pope from any point on the globe. The Dome records the great technological progress of humanity. It also poses the question whether the then unthinkable developments made by science can be used to benefit humankind as a whole.

Most recognised of the costs of human development has been the damage done to the environment and the reckless use of the earth's resources. In wondering at the exhibits contained within the Dome it is easy to miss some of the important techno-ecological adjustments involved in the structure's creation. The large rotund blue and steely grey round towers which surround the building are part of a huge water recycling project which ensures that the Dome collects the rain water from its twenty five acre roof, as well as water used inside, and re-uses it. London's water table is rising and the Dome, despite coping with 35,000 visitors a day, will not add to the problem.

Exhibits will display how materials can be recycled. One of the zones is a structure built of re-enforced cardboard strong enough to be stood upon. The invention of Japanese scientist, Shigeru Ban, the cardboard enabled rescue workers in the Kobe earthquake disaster to erect emergency homes within hours. Also on display is a complete wall made from crushed drinks cans sent in by children. The Dome organisers will also be recycling their plastic cups on site and making pencils for the organisers and visitors. For the refrigerators only environmentally friendly hydrocarbons will be used.

MILLENNIUM DOME

The land on which the Dome was built was once a gas works. It was derelict, much of it toxic. The land has been cleaned up and will also house The Millennium Village which will have 1,400 homes with shops.

Building the Dome

On a loop of the Thames in North Greenwich, the land had lain waste for many years. Once an industrial site, it had been victim to the dumping policies of industry. Almost a decade ago foreign journalists were contacting Greenwich council to request details and seats at the local millennium celebrations. They concluded that Greenwich, as the home of time, would be the centre of a huge celebration of the oncoming of the third millennium. An idea was born. Greenwich had the waste land to accommodate a large complex near the capital, as well as the historic connection.

The government decided that Greenwich would be the focus of Britain's millennium celebrations. The decision was not without controversy. Manchester and Birmingham also bid to hold the festival. Many people thought that the millennium would be celebrated by investing in much needed hospitals and schools. But Greenwich won out and construction began in June, 1997 when the first of 8,000 concrete piles were driven into the ground.

The design was the idea of Mike Davis, one of the Dome's architects, who was inspired by a national exhibition which he had visited 40 years previously. He recreated the image of a dome. Otherwise the Dome's design is entirely pragmatic with no formal declaration of art other than that it is the model of practical architecture to come. Our search for a meaning for our millennium creation ended up with an earthy response.

We were informed that one of the great master's of Feng Shui opined that the feminine mound of the Dome is in beautiful symmetry to the phallic Canada House which stands across the Thames in Canary Wharf.

A six metre wide ring of reinforced concrete was installed to encircle the Dome anchoring the steel cables which would each support 20 tons of roof. Twelve 90 metre masts were erected in October of the same year reaching 100 metres into the sky. The following month 72 paired radial cables supporting the canopy netting were winched up. From here 80 mountaineers at any one time were abseiling down to put up high strength cable.

By March, 1998 the first fabric panels of the 150 ton roof were being put up. Made of Teflon coated glass fibre and woven, they formed a double layer spanning 100,000 square metres of roofing insulating the interior. The structure was finally completed in June 1998. Barely one year after building had begun, the prime minister, Tony Blair, was able to attend the Topping Out ceremony.

Health and safety were major considerations in construction. On visiting the site we were taken into a cloakroom to don our helmets, luminous waste jackets and Wellington boots. We could see cleaners vacuuming the gantry high above the arena. Equipped with masks and gloves they were also protected by a lunge attached to their backs. If they suffered from a sudden attack of vertigo (for which they had undergone hours of training) the lunge would prevent them from hitting the ground.

One of the proudest achievements of those creating the Dome is that after 600,000 man hours of work on site not one major industrial accident had occurred.

As for that hole.........

One of the most surprising aspects of the design is the large hole in the Dome which can be seen from the Thames and when entering from North Greenwich station. According to the organisers the hole allows for two ducts emitting fumes from the Blackwall Tunnel which passes beneath the site and under the Thames. The organisers say that had the Dome been moved slightly up or down river it would have ended up in the Thames. Had it been moved away from the river it would have scuppered plans for the Millennium Village. The hole was a compromise.

The two ducts are closed off to visitors. Should you get the chance to see them they are quite attractive pieces of engineering and did really deserve a place as a touch of reality in the grand theme park.

MILLENNIUM DOME

Aside from the ethical considerations the Dome is also fantastic fun. The centre piece of the Dome is the huge arena. With its columns and raised seating it appeared to us reminiscent of the Coliseum in Rome. 4,500 people can be seated around here to watch the daily shows put on by performers from around the world. A hundred and twenty metres up, windows at the core of the roof open and shut bringing air and light. The whole construction is an excellent blending of curves, lines, spirals and circles which are surprisingly pleasing to the eye.

Some of the most creative individuals in the world of live entertainment are supervising the shows. Architect **Mark Fisher**, who has worked with Pink Floyd, U2, REM and the Rolling Stones is the Show Creative Director. Co-founder of Genesis and creator of an innovative school blending musical trends from around the world, Peter Gabriel, is the Music Director. Also in the team is Greenwich's very own jazz musician, **Jools Holland**.

On the perimeter of the Dome are 14 theme zones, each housing so many attractions that it will be a test of stamina to visit them all in one day. Visitors need to prioritise their attractions. When we visited the zones were still being constructed. Entering the Dome, the first zone encountered is the Work and **Learning Zone**. With huge 11-metre high triptych rotating boards, the structure has a ground floor with interactive exhibits concerning work methods in the past and the skills required in the third millennium. On the upper floor one is encouraged to learn, moving from the school of the past down a corridor to the **Learning Orchard of the Future**.

I was most attracted by the **Mind Zone**. At the time it was a huge mass of terracotta girders, erected as the base for a huge platform to extend unsupported towards the arena. Eminent engineers had predicted that the concept of designer Zaha Hadid was so fantastic that it could not be realised. See for yourself.

The transparent blue panels of the structure are lit from below to give an electric feel with continually folding surfaces and a 32 metre high central screen. Inside is a feast of optical illusions, sculptures and the latest technology to explore the wondrous workings of the human brain.

Another potential favourite is the **Body Zone**. When we arrived it was a mass of steel poles, the frame for a huge building in the shape of two entwined human bodies. The steel substructure was later encased in glass-reinforced concrete and covered with tiles. Walk around the reclining lovers and see how their colour changes. Step inside through the thirty-metre hip of one of the figures, and climb the escalators of the twenty seven metre high abstract, and you will feel like you are inside the human body. You will also find interactive exhibits on health, beauty, lifestyle and medical discoveries revealing the marvellous workings of *homo sapiens*.

Next door to the Body Zone is the kid's **Play Zone** with a host of the latest interactive games. It's a recommended zone for fathers who can take their kids as an excuse to play. One guaranteed favourite for the old boys is the virtual reality game allowing the viewer to pit their penalty-taking skills against the best goalkeepers in world soccer.

The wall of the **Living Island Zone** is constructed from recycled drink cans and is entered via a sewage pipe. Inside, however, is another fun place for kids, with a pebbled beach, promenade, and games arcade. It's a seaside scenario with plenty of learning facilities with regard to the coastal environment.

The attractive, spiralling **Shared Ground Zone** inspired by Shigeru Ban features the world's largest structure made from recycled cardboard, and 14 metre high columns form the perimeter. They were created from cardboard sent in by tens of thousands of children. The zone is devoted to community and explores personal space in the cities. An associated theme of communication is highlighted in the **Talk Zone**, with its two six-storey high pavilions of 'live skins' talking to each other.

New travel solutions and virtual travel are the main themes of the **Journey Zone** which is housed in a spectacular structure, with 25 metre high angled fins covered in flashing lights shooting high into the air. Once again interactive in content, the quickest way of getting to see what you want is to strap on the virtual goggles and fly off around the world. Other interactive exhibits allow visitors to deal with the dilemmas facing today's town planners, trying to assess the impact of pedestrianising streets, creating bus lanes and charging drivers for city centre access. The latest environmentally friendly technology and transport prototypes are also on display.

Next step was the **Home Planet Zone**. Floating high above was a giant globe. Surrounding visitors will be a unique shimmering blue building in which one can take a trip through space and at the same time drop back onto earth to view some of its most incredible phenomena. It offers the only real ride in the Dome. And beyond space, the controversial **Faith Zone** whose main sponsor is the Hinduja Foundation. The celebration of the millennium is more a celebration of human achievement than anything related to the life and lectures of a young carpenter in Palestine. In the year 1000 AD, the Christian faith dominated Europe and its high priests ruled the land. In today's secular, democratic Britain more Moslems attend the mosque than Christians attend church.

The best thing about the **Money Zone** is that visitors can play at being tycoons in an interactive game. For one day in your life you can be one of those people who move your money around the world, affecting your job, your home and your government. After this you might want to visit the 14 metre high circular **Self Portrait Zone**. Its revolving facade, Andscape, portrays images sent in by the public depicting how the British see themselves. Inside is a huge collage, **National Portrait**, which is the work of David Mach, and monstrous sculptures by the fabulous cartoonist Gerald Scarfe.

Before leaving the zones inside the Dome, visitors are invited to take a nap in the Rest Zone. It's actually on the inner ring of the zones and suitably close to the Mind Zone. The aim is to stimulate your ability to relax and the hope is

MILLENNIUM DOME

that you will be refreshed sufficiently by the zone to keep going around the other attractions outside. The setting is a huge coloured bubble with seating, soothing lights and piped music

McDonald's may be a controversial sponsor but their Our Town Stage just outside the Dome is a marvellous 500-seat theatre topped by black and white fantasy spirals. Children from communities around Britain are visiting the theatre with its three shows a day to tell the story of their towns. Another symbol of the 90s, Sky Television, are the sponsors of both of the 2,500-seat Skyscape cinemas, featuring a thirty minute film on Blackadder. The **Entertainment Zone** is the 15th zone and also lies outside the Dome canopy.

For those seeking rest and refreshment there are 30 **bars** and **restaurants**, with a range of popular names including Harry Ramsdens and McDonald's. **Disabled access** is guaranteed from North Greenwich station right into the Dome.

After the Dome, What Next?

The Dome is set to be a festival exhibition centre for one year but the structure is such that it could last for another three hundred years. It is expected to last 25 years without major maintenance. In 1999 the government were inviting suggestions for the structure's future use. Local football club Charlton Athletic suggested that it would make a nice new stadium for them. The Chinese Embassy thought it might make an excellent trade centre. Other ideas included a permanent exhibition to new technology, a concert hall, a Disney centre, an indoor cricket ground and a film studio. It could otherwise provide a testing golf circuit as no golfer yet has been found who can hit a ball across the Dome's perimeter.

At the very least its construction would have accelerated the development of Greenwich by bringing forward the building of new roads, rail tracks and environmental projects and making the borough one of the most desirous tourist locations in the country.

The stylish way to get to the Dome is to take one of the many river boats down the Thames past landmarks including the Tower of London and Canary Wharf, alighting at the site. Getting there by car means parking somewhere outside Greenwich and taking a bus or train. Parking is restricted to orange badge holders only within three kilometres of the site. The site however has parking space for three hundred coaches and taxis may drop and collect passengers.

On the Underground, North Greenwich tube on the Jubilee Line is right by Gate 3 of the Dome. This part of the Jubilee line can be accessed in North London by taking the Docklands Light Railway's driverless trains to Canning Town and changing. Rail passengers arriving from the south and from the European continent at Waterloo International can reach North Greenwich in 12 minutes. For overland rail the main alighting station will be Charlton where buses will run frequently to the site. The 108 bus also runs every ten minutes between Charlton, Blackheath and Greenwich District Hospital. Bus 477 runs frequently to Plumstead and Woolwich. Buses also run to other parts of Greenwich and south east London.

Cyclists and walkers can reach the Dome from the Thames Barrier and Deptford via the Riverside Walk beside the Thames. Motorcyclists will not be restricted from riding to the Dome.

Listings

Accommodation

All accommodation listed here has been checked by London Tourist Board except those with 'ETB Applied' next to them.

Hotels
Greenwich
Hotel Ibis ** (0208 305 1177 fax 858 7139) 30 Stockwell St.
The Mitre Hotel (0208 293 0037 fax 355 6761, disability access) 291 Greenwich High Rd – ETB 2 Crowns Commended.
Greenwich Parkhouse Hotel (0208 305 1478) Nevada St.

Blackheath
Clarendon Hotel ** (0208 318 4321 fax 4378) Montpelier Row, ETB 3 Crowns Approved.
Bardon Lodge (0208 853 4051) 15 Stratheden Rd – ETB 3 Crowns Commended.
Vanbrugh Hotel (0208 853 4051) 21 St Johns Park, ETB Applied.
Cactus Hotel (0208 852 0883) Blackheath Village.

Eltham
Meadowcroft Lodge (0208 859 1488) 96 Southwood Rd, New Eltham.
Weston House Hotel (0208 850 5191) 8 Eltham Green – ETB 1 Crown Approved.
Yardley Court Hotel (0208 850 1850 fax 488 0421) 18 Court Yard – ETB 2 Crowns Commended.

Bed & Breakfast
Greenwich
Trinity Cottage, Trinity Grove (0208 469 2017) ETB Applied.
69 Ashburnum Place (0208 692 9065) ETB Applied.

81 Greenwich South St (0208 293 3121) ETB Listed Highly Commended.
77 Lassell St (0208 858 9388) ETB Applied
Binnie Court, 40 Greenwich High Rd (0208 694 2789) Self Catering (Summer Only).
51 Hyde Vale (0208 692 9677) ETB 3 Keys. Self catering Only.

Blackheath
59A Lee Rd (0208 318 7244) ETB Listed Commended.
59 Lee Terrace (0208 852 6334 mobile 0961 900455) ETB Applied.
68 Wricklemarsh Rd (0208 856 1331) ETB Listed Approved.
Wayside, Heathway (0208 858 5088) ETB Applied.
29 Tellison Avenue, Shooters Hill Rd (0208 856 9213 mobile 07930 173613) ETB Listed Approved.
135 Shooters Hill Rd (0208 858 1420) Self Catering.
268 Shooters Hill Rd (0208 319 2699) ETB Listed Approved.
Magpie Lodge, 26 Shooters Hill Rd (0208 858 3953 mobile 00831 300167) ETB Listed Highly Commended.
Number Nine, 9 Charlton Rd (0208 858 4175 mobile 07957 361997) ETB Listed Commended.
64 Beaconsfield Rd (0208 858 1685) ETB Applied.
49 Foxes Dale (0208 852 1076 mobile 0370 583487) ETB Applied.

Eltham
70 Dunvegan Rd (0208 850 0584) ETB Applied.
68 Dunvegan Rd (0208 859 3924) ETB Listed Commended.
50 Beechill Rd (0208 850 4863) ETB Applied.
80 Rennets Rd (0208 850 1829).

LISTINGS

Oakfield, 36 Southend Crescent
(0208 859 8989) ETB 2 Crowns Highly
Commended.
Benvenuti, 217 Court Rd
(0208 857 4855 fax 265 5635)
ETB Listed Highly Commended.
33 Glenshiel Rd (0208 850 4958)
ETB Listed Commended.

Charlton
Pickwick Hotel (0208 858 0324
fax 5532) 246 Woolwich Rd, Charlton.

Kidbrooke
3 Tilbrook Rd (0208 319 8843)
ETB Listed Approved.

Plumstead
Acacia Parade, 302 Plumstead Common
(0208 855 2969) ETB Listed
Commended.

Youth and Groups
Binnie Court, 40 Greenwich High Rd
(0208 694 2789).
Rotherhithe Youth Hostel (0207 232
2114) Salter Rd, Rotherhithe, SE16

Camping & Caravans
Abbey Wood Caravan Club
(0208 310 2233 fax 311 6007)
Federation Rd, Abbey Wood.

Restaurants & Cafés
Greenwich
Trafalgar Tavern (0208 858 2437
Fax 0208 858 2507) Park Row.
Old Royal Naval College Coffee Shop
Park Cafe (0870 8422246)
Greenwich Park.
Royal Teas (Vegetarian)
(0208 691 7240) 76 Royal Hill.
Davys Wine Vaults (0208 858 7204)
165 Greenwich High Rd.
Colonel Jaspers (0208 853 0585)
161 Greenwich High Rd.
North Pole (0208 853 3020)
131 Greenwich High Rd.

Kum Luang (Thai) (0208 293 4011)
326 Creek Rd.
Vietnam Restaurant (0208 858 0871)
17 King William Walk.
The Tea House (0208 858 0803)
14 King William Walk.
Thyme Restaurant (0208 293 9183)
1A Station Crescent.
Cafe Rouge (French) (0208 293 6660)
30 Stockwell St.
Spread Eagle (French) (0208 853 2333)
2 Stockwell St.
Green Village (0208 858 2348)
11Greenwich Church St.
Mogul Tandoori (Nepalese) (0208
858 1500) 10 Greenwich Church St.
Halomama Noodle Bar (0208 293 5263)
10 Nelson Rd.
Thai Chung (0208 858 8588)
8 Nelson Rd.
Café Sol (0208 853 4385)
13 Nelson Rd.
Saigon (Vietnamese) (0208 853 0414)
16 Nelson Rd.
Googies (Vegetarian)
19 Greenwich South St.
Escaped Café (Vegetarian) (0208
692 5826) 141 Greenwich South St.
Millennium Balti House
(0208 293 5464) 17 Collomb St.
Othello Steak & Kebab House (Greek)
(0208 858 7050) 113 Trafalgar Rd.

Blackheath
Regent Palace (Chinese)
(0208 318 0791) 5 Lee Rd.
El Pirata (Spanish) (0208 297 1880)
15 Royal Parade.
Chapter Two (0208 333 2666)
43 Montpelier Vale.
Cactus Pit (Mexican/Texan)
(0208 852 0883) 10 Royal Parade.
Ciao Bellina (Italian) (0208 852 9226)
17 Montpelier Vale.
Clarendon Hotel (0208 318 4321)
Montpelier Row.
Lawn (0207 379 0724)
1 Lawn Terrace

LISTINGS

Café Italia (0208 858 7577)
107 Humber Rd, Westcombe Park.
Marinus Restaurant (fish)
(0208 318 2116) 121 Lee Rd.

Eltham
Mellins Wine Bar and Restaurant
(0208 850 4462)
Eltham High St.
Electric Café (0208 859 4095)
183 Eltham High St.
Tudor Barn, Well Hall Pleasance
(0208 850 5145), Well Hall Rd.
Brasseria Napoli (0208 850 8102)
21 Elm Terrace.
Eltham Grill House (0208 859 0807)
2 Chequers Parade.
Jaya House Malaysian & Chinese
Restaurant (0208 857 2188)
754 Sidcup Rd, New Eltham.
Lale Restaurant (Turkish & French)
(0208 850 1462) 66 High St.
Le Dolomiti (Italian) (0208 850 3332)
747 Sidcup Rd, New Eltham.
Mahathma Tandoori (0208 859 7954)
156 Bexley Rd, Avery Hill.
Oriental Garden (0208 850 9889)
12 Well Hall Rd.
Pizza Hut (0208 850 9977)
190 Eltham High St.
Raymonds Pie, Eel & Mash Shop
(Traditional East London)
(0208 850 9062) 10 Passey Place.
Three Cooks (0208 850 5219)
114 High St.
Wimpy (Fast Food) (0208 850 8801)
95 Eltham High St.

Charlton
Floyds Bar (0208 293 4567)
The Valley, Charlton Athletic.
The Thames Barrier Visitors Centre
(0208 845 1373) Unity Way.
Wing Chings (Vietnamese)
(0208 269 1029), Charlton Church Lane.
The Valley Café, Charlton Church Lane.
Taste of Raj (0208 319 3439)
10 The Village.

Woolwich
The Place (0208 316 7533)
32A Hare St.
Il Traghetto (0208 854 8710)
123 Woolwich High St
Pizza Hut (0208 854 4460)
83 Powis St.
Sukan Vegetarian Restaurant,
13 Anglesea Rd.
Wimpy (Fast Food) (0208 317 8746)
22 Thomas St
Frans Café (0208 858 3883)
257 Woolwich Rd.

Plumstead
Goan Cuisine (0208 317 1966)
136 Plumstead High St.
Kanchans Vegetarian Restaurant
62 Plumstead High St.
Taste of Punjab (0208 855 8725)
2 Plumstead High St.

Entertainment

Greenwich
Greenwich Theatre (0208 858 7755)
Crooms Hill.
Princes Theatre (0208 969 2910)
189 Greenwich High Rd.
Greenwich Dance Agency
(0208 293 9741) Royal Hill.
Up The Creek Comedy Club
(0208 858 4581) Creek Road..
Park Cafe (0870 8422246)
Greenwich Park – Jazz.
St Alfege Church (choral music) (0870
900 0355) Greenwich Church St
Greenwich Cinema (0208 235 3005)
180 Greenwich High Rd.

Blackheath
Blackheath Concert Halls
(0208 463 0100) 23 Lee Rd.
The Green Club (0208 468 7648)
Royal Parade, Jazz, Thurs eves.
Kingswood Halls (0208 852 0234).
Age Exchange Cinema Club and New
Youth Theatre (0208 318 9105)
11 Blackheath Village.

Blackheath Conservatoire of Music and the Arts (0208 852 0234) 19 Lee Rd.

Eltham
Bob Hope Theatre (0208 850 3702) Wythfield Rd.
TopRank (Bingo) (0208 850 3767).

Woolwich
Woolwich Public Hall
(0208 317 0819) Market St.
Odeon Coronet Cinema
(0181 854 2255) John Wilson St.
Gala Clubs (Bingo) (020 854 2678) 186 Powis St.
The Old Tramshed (Comedy Club), Off Wilmot St.

Plumstead
Greenwich & Lewisham Young Peoples Theatre (0208 845 1316) Burrage Rd.

Pubs with Live Music
Greenwich
Cutty Sark Tavern (0208 858 3146). Ballast Quay, Tues, Thurs, Fri evenings and Sundays.
Trafalgar Tavern (0208 858 2437 fax 0208 8582507) Park Row.
The Cricketers Arms (0208 858 3630) King William Walk, English folk Tues nights, New Orleans jazz Sunday afternoons.
Funnel and Firkin pub
(0208 305 2088)
174 Greenwich High Rd.
Prince of Orange pub (0208 488 7123) 188 Greenwich High Rd.
Rick's Bar & Restaurant
(0208 858 1032) 208 Trafalgar Rd, Jazz Saturday nights.
King William IV (0208 858 0656) 155 Trafalgar Rd. Fri, Sat and Sunday afternoon.
Lord Hood (0208 858 1836)
300 Creek Rd, Fri & Sat Disco.

Blackheath
Fairway and Firkin, Blackheath Village

Art Exhibitions & Museums
Greenwich
National Maritime Museum, Old Royal Observatory & Queens House
(0208 858 4422) Greenwich Park.
Royal Naval College (0208 858 2154) King William Walk.
Greenwich Village Gallery
(0208 858 2290) 7 Turnpin Lane.
Harlequin Gallery (0208 692 7170) 68 Greenwich High Rd.
Fan Museum (0208 858 7879)
12 Crooms Hill.
Cutty Sark (0208 858 3445)
Ballast Quay.
Fergus Noone Photography
(0208 858 3309) Greenwich Market.

Blackheath
Blackheath Gallery (0208 852 1802).
Rangers House (0208 853 0035) Chesterfield Walk.
Woodlands Art Gallery (0208 858 5847) 90 Mycenae Rd.

Woolwich
Citizens' Gallery (0208 316 2736) 151 Powis St.
The Royal Artillery Rotunda Museum
(0208 316 5402) Repository Rd.

Plumstead
Borough Museum (0208 855 3240) 232 Plumstead High St.

Eltham
Eltham Palace (0208 294 2548)
Court Yard.

Charlton
Charlton House (0208 858 7809), The Village...

Markets
Greenwich Market (0208 293 3110) College Approach. Fri-Sun, arts & crafts; Thurs, antiques.

Stockwell Market, Stockwell St,
Sat & Sun
Woolwich Market, Beresford Market
Square, Mon-Sat, 2pm closing on Thurs.
Plumstead Covered Market, Plumstead
Rd, Mon – Sat, 2pm closing on Thurs.
Thomas Tallis School Toy Collectors'
Fair (0208 859 3242)
Kidbrooke Park Rd, SE3, Sundays.

Summer Kids Events

Arches Leisure Centre (0208 317 5000)
Trafalgar Rd Greenwich. Creche,
children's pool sessions, kid's club,
rookie lifeguards course, gym club, step
class, toddler's world.
Charlton Lido (0208 856 7180)
Charlton Park Lane, Charlton.
50 metre pool, children's splash pool,
fun sessions.
The Valley
(0208 853 5454)
The Valley, Charlton.
Creche, fitness room
sessions.
Millennium Fitness Centre
(0208 850 1234) Messter
Place, Eltham.
Creche, fitness room
sessions.
Eltham Pools
(0208 859 0898)
Eltham Hill. Fun sessions,
pool disco, diving boards,
rookie lifeguard courses,
family splashes.
Plumstead Leisure Centre
(0208 855 8289) Speranza
St, Plumstead. Creche,
goalkeeping and
football sessions, basketball, roller-skating, table
tennis, trampolining.
Thamesmere Leisure
Centre
(0208 311 1119)
Thamesmere Drive,
Thamesmead. Creche,

toddlers world, pool disco, summer
playscheme, under-fives pool, gym club,
swim school.
Waterfront Leisure Centre
(0208 317 5000) Woolwich High St
Creche, toddlers pool, hot tub, swim
school, basketball, football, adventure
playzone.
Coldharbour Leisure Centre (0208 851
8692) Chapel Farm Rd, New Eltham
Summer Soccer School, creche,
playscheme, toddlers world, netball.
Woodlands Farm (0208 319 8900)
331 Shooters Hill Rd. Farming Centre.

Guided Tours

Greenwich Tour Guides Association
(0870 608200) Pepys House, Cutty Sark
Gardens, Greenwich.

(Courtesy Blackheath Halls)

Musician and TV presenter Jools Holland

LISTINGS

Recommended Reading

For those visitors who want to know more about the borough, there are several books on the history of the borough. These include:

Blackheath Village And Its Environs by Neil Rhind (Bookshop Blackheath).

The Story of Greenwich by Clive Aslet (Fourth Estate).

Royal Greenwich by Oliver Nigel Hamilton (Greenwich Bookshop).

Greenwich Marsh – The 300 Years Before The Dome by Mary Mills (M.Wright)

Darrell Spurgeon has written several comprehensive architectural guides published by Greenwich Guide Books on parts of the borough and its surrounds. These include:

Discover Woolwich And Its Environs

Discover Greenwich And Charlton

Discover Eltham

Discover Erith and Crayford (includes Thamesmead)

Discover Lewisham and Deptford

Other pamphlets of interest available from **Greenwich Local History Library** (tel. 0208 858 4631) include:

Woodlands and John Julius Angerstein by Sally Jenkinson.

Chesterfield Walk: Three Georgian Houses by Sally Jenkinson (includes Ranger's House, McCartney House and Montague House)

Free For All: A celebration of 100 years of the Woolwich Free Ferry by Julian Watson and Wendy Gregory.

Sugar Spices And Human Cargo: An Early Black History Of Greenwich by Joan Anim-Addo

Black History in Greenwich by Julian Watson

The History of Abbey Wood by C.R.Jarvis (includes Lesnes Abbey)

Other titles in MH*i*'s pleasure seeking guides series

Hidden Kerala: the travel guide

The acclaimed comprehensive guide to south India's paradise state. Phil Frampton and Steffanie Kalt travel from Kovalam Beach, through the cities of Kerala, and along the famous backwaters on a journey of discovery to the region's wilds, mountains and valleys. *Price £9.95.*

Emilia Romagna: Italy's hidden gem

All and more of what the traveller needs to know about Tuscany's prosperous and relatively tourist-free neighbour which embraces some of Italy's most picturesque and historic cities including Bologna, Parma, Ferrara, Ravenna and Rimini, and their tranquil countryside. *Price £13.95.*

Available from MHi Publications Ltd, 44 Grindley Ave, Manchester M21 7NF.

READING

Index

INDEX

About the Author

Phil Frampton works as a journalist and research consultant. Educated at Bristol University, his work has taken him across four continents. Author of the acclaimed travel guide, *Hidden Kerala*, he has also written on travel and other issues for the *Guardian*, *Independent on Sunday, Wanderlust* and a variety of international papers.

Your say

When you've visited Greenwich, you'll have your own impressions, likes and dislikes. Your comments will be invaluable to us especially if you have new discoveries, different insights and tales to tell. Share them with us and we'll share them with others who might be thinking of travelling to Greenwich.

If you would like more copies of this book for you or your friends, send a cheque or postal order for £10.95 per book with your address to MH*i* Publications, 44 Grindley Avenue, Manchester, M21 7NF.